Social Media Marketing

How to Build and Execute Your Own Social Media Strategy

3rd Edition

M.J. BROWN

Social Media Marketing

Table of Contents

Introduction

I want to thank you and congratulate you for purchasing the book, *"Social Media Marketing"*.

This book contains proven steps and strategies on how to use social media to market your products and services.

Social media has evolved rapidly and turned into an important part of our life and how the world functions. Only a few years ago people said that if as a business, you are not on social media, you are missing out. Today nobody says that because it's a given that every business, no matter how big or small, has an online presence. It's no longer just an additional source of leads or just a side note in the marketing plan of a business. Social media is now at the centre stage of how businesses run and how they market their products and services.

It's not just big businesses, that can invest a lot of money in their online marketing, that benefit from social media. There are thousands of inspiring stories about small businesses that are successful only because of their online presence and social media marketing strategy.

Thousands of indie artists, musicians, writers, and creators of all kind are making a living doing what they love, because of the internet. Even more people have started small businesses that are completely online and completely automated and earn quite a decent amount of passive income. All they do is market their business on social media and keep earning week after week.

There is no denying the power of social media. We spend most of our time on one or the other social network. We get our news from social media. We search online for products. We search online for reviews of restaurants we want to eat in. The biggest market in the world today is the virtual marketplace on the internet. You can sell anything to anyone, anywhere in the world. And if you know how to use social media marketing, you can build a business from scratch for a fraction of the capital required to start a brick and mortar business.

The world of social media moves incredibly fast. Search engines and social networks continuously change the rules of the game and tactics and strategies change to keep up with the new rules. It can be overwhelming to stay on top of all of these changes on all of the social networks, all the time. But no matter how quickly things change, the basics remain the same. This book is focused on the basics of social media marketing that will teach you how to adapt to every change that will happen in the future. If you stick to the basics, the rest is easy.

This book is divided into 3 parts. In the first part we'll talk about what social media marketing is and how to build your own social media marketing strategy. In the second part we'll discuss several social media networks in detail so you can choose the best ones for your strategy. In the third and final part we'll discuss how to execute and manage your strategy.

In this book you'll learn:

- The basics of social media marketing.

- How to form a good social media strategy.

- How to start a good blog that will be the cornerstone of your social media empire.

- How to optimize your strategy on sites such as Facebook, Twitter, Google+, LinkedIn, YouTube, Pinterest, Instagram etc.

- How to execute and manage the system without getting overwhelmed by it.

Thanks again for purchasing this book, I hope you enjoy it!

M.J. Brown

Part 1
Social Media Marketing Strategy

Chapter 1

A Crash Course on Social Media Marketing

The internet has become the main focus of all marketers. Print and TV advertisements now point to the website and social accounts of the company. The entire marketing campaign for any company, no matter how big or small, is tied around the company's web presence. But why is this so?

Just think about how many people are connected to the internet today. Almost the entire consumer base is present online and it spends a lot of time online. The mobile phone revolution shrunk the entire world into a globalized society and the advent of smart phones has connected the entire world by bringing the internet in the palms of our hands. There are more than a billion users just on Facebook.

The numbers alone are baffling but now think about what these people do on the internet. They connect with family, friends, strangers and colleagues, and they talk about their lives. They share jokes, news, photographs and videos. And they talk about products. Every marketer will tell you that the best type of marketing is "word of mouth" marketing.

When you hear about a product from someone you personally know, you automatically have more trust than if you were watching an advertisement on television. Social media marketing results in this type of word of mouth publicity that has a much bigger impact on prospective consumers than any other form of marketing. It also has the possibility of growing exponentially by going viral.

We've all heard about viral videos that reached millions of viewers in a few days. This potential to go viral is also why all marketers now focus a lot of social media. And on top of all that, it's one of the cheapest forms of marketing. Can a small business make a high quality television commercial and buy a prime time spot? Probably not. But for a fraction of that money a small business can create a presence on social networks, engage a community and advertise to them. Considering the fact that we all change the channel whenever an ad comes on, social media is not just the cheaper option but also the more effective one.

So What Actually *IS* Social Media Marketing?

Social media marketing is a way of gaining traffic to your website through the use of social media sites. Marketing efforts in this area tend to concentrate on creating content that attracts the attention of their chosen audience and encouraging them to share it with all their friends and followers across social media. The result is an electronic word of mouth that spreads fast, earning the marketer good media visibility for next to no outlay.

Social media websites work by letting people interact with each other and build up relationships. When a business joins in, it allows potential customers to interact directly with them, creating a more personal touch and ensuring that customers are likely to pass the word about you on to their friends and families. And, because they are sharing your news with their friends, more people get to see it and pass it on to their friends, and so on, resulting in an increase in traffic that may convert to sales.

Social media marketing is used by more than 70% of today's businesses and has resulted in an increase of more than 130% in revenue. It isn't only computers that are used for surfing the internet; mobile phones and tablets are now used much more for accessing social media websites than they ever have been. Most smartphones have social media apps enabled and people are notified immediately when anything happens on their social media sites. This is a constant connection that allows businesses to keep their customers fully in the loop about what's happening and what's new.

Social Media Strategies

There are two main strategies that businesses should use with social media marketing:

The Passive Approach

Social media is a very useful source of information and customer voices for business. There are plenty of places where people share their views and their brand recommendations and business owners can tap into these and look at what the customer wants. In this sense, social media marketing is a cheap way of tapping into market intelligence, which is then used by the business to track down problems and opportunities. Let's take an example – the iPhone 6 Plus, released in September 2014.

The internet boiled over with videos of the newest handset from Apple undergoing a bend test after it was alleged that the handset could be bent by hand. This created no small amount of confusion amongst those who had been waiting for months for this new iPhone to be launched. Did Apple ignore it? No. They came straight back with a statement to say that this was a rare occurrence and they uploaded a video shot in their own torture room, showing the iPhone 6 being put through a rigorous series of tests. As you can see, social media can now be used to get a live reaction to a product or service, making it extremely useful to any marketer.

Social Media Marketing

The Active Approach

We can also use social media as a channel of communication and a way of engaging the public. There are quite a few companies who use some kind of dialogue online to build relationships with their customers, including the likes of Jonathon Swartz, CEO and President of Sun Microsystems and Bob Langert, Vice President of McDonalds. The idea is to encourage people to express their views, their ideas and pass on suggestions and using influences like this can be an extremely cost effective method of marketing.

Advertising

Whether you choose the active or the passive approach, the key to social media marketing, of course comes down to advertising. That's the main purpose of any marketing campaign: to sell stuff. You can advertise on the internet in the form of banners that will be seen on other websites, landing pages on your own websites, google ads that will place your products on search engine pages and marketing on social networks such as Facebook and Twitter.

The Basics

The first requirement is to have an online presence. Whether you are a big company or a small startup, whether you are part of an organization or an individual, you need to have an online presence. Online presence simply means to set up shop in the virtual world. Think of it as a shop, a store, an office, or even a virtual basement that you work out of. This will be a website or a blog. This is the place where you'll send all your customers to find out more about your products or services and to buy what you are selling.

Along with a website, you need to be active on at least a few social networks. There are thousands of networks to choose from but you should only use as many as you can manage properly. There are the good old social networks such as Facebook, Twitter and Google+. There are video sharing sites such as YouTube and Vimeo. There are picture sharing sites such as Pinterest and Instagram. There are sites like Reddit, Scribd, Slideshare that allow you to curate and share other form of content. The type of product or service you are selling and the type of content you can create, will dictate the type of social network that you use.

Go where your audience is. Create what your audience wants.

Once you have the basic setup of a website/blog and a few social networks you can start engaging with people. Here's where the difference from traditional marketing starts. Unlike traditional marketing, this is not a one way communication channel. You can't just broadcast promotional content all the time and not interact with your audience. If you try to do this, you'll soon drive everyone away.

Instead, in social media marketing you need to listen to what others are saying. You need to have real communication with your audience. And most importantly, you need to provide real value to your audience. It's not "*buy my product and you'll receive this much value.*" It's more like "*here's all this free value for you and if you want more you can buy my product.*"

If you can understand this "catch" of social media marketing, then you'll be able to fully utilize it.

A lot of traditional marketers get into social media with their old habits. They only focus on building numbers and promoting their products endlessly to these numbers. They opt for quantity over quality. This approach doesn't work on social media and can actually have a negative effect. You should focus on quality instead of quantity. Even if you have a few hundred followers but all of them are dedicate fans of your product, you are in a much better situation than someone who has a hundred thousand followers but none of them really care about the product.

You can use tools for analyzing your social media outreach and see the kind of impact different content has on your audience. This ability to analyze your data is unique to social media marketing and it can prove to be very powerful. You can then tailor your content to suit exactly what your audience wants.

What Can You Do With Social Media?

If you have an online presence and are active on a few social networks and have a quality audience you can do the following:

1. Sell your products to your audience.

This is the main goal of any type of marketing. When you sell to a hand picked audience all of whom have shown an interest in your product, the chances of making a sale increase a lot. All other forms of advertising are intrusive and force themselves on the audience. You sit down to watch your favorite movie and someone interrupts you and tries to sell you something. Obviously, your first reaction will be of annoyance and maybe even anger. But in social media marketing, you create a relationship with your audience and you advertise in front of only those people who have shown an interest in you. So the conversion rates can be much higher than other traditional types of marketing.

2. Ask your audience to help you spread the word.

This is possible only with social media marketing and if you have developed strong relationships with your audience they won't mind doing this work for you at all. If your product has provided them value and you have shown that you listen to your audience then they'll happily become missionaries for your product, spreading your name wherever they go.

Social Media Marketing

3. Listen to your audience to help improve your products and services.

This is an immense value proposition of social media marketing. Usually companies pay customers to participate in surveys so that they can develop better products. But on social media, you get constant feedback from your audience and if used intelligently, it will help you offer the best value to your audience.

4. Provide great customer service to build a strong brand image.

Social media is great for providing quick customer service to anyone who has a complaint or question. If done right, it will put you in a rare league of companies that actually care about their customers. Keep your customers happy and they'll talk about you with their friends.

5. Give your customers the opportunity to help you develop your business.

It's called crowdfunding. If you have a strong connection with your audience, it can actually help you raise money without having to go to traditional sources for a loan. This is way beyond any kind of traditional marketing.

These are some of the main things you can achieve through social media marketing. If there's just one thing you should remember, then it is that social media marketing will work well if you genuinely care about providing value to your audience. Keep this mantra in mind and you'll master social media marketing in no time.

Top 15 Most Popular Social Networking Sites

The number of social networking sites continues to grow as each year passes. These are the top 15 as of 2015, complete with an estimation of unique visitors per month:

1. Facebook – 900,000,000

2. Twitter – 310,000,000

3. LinkedIn – 255,000,000

4. Pinterest – 250,000,000

5. Google+ - 120,000,000

6. Tumblr – 110,000,000

7. Instagram – 100,000,000

8. VK – 80,000,000

9. Flickr – 65,000,000

10. Vine – 42,000,000

11. Meetup – 40,000,000

12. Tagged – 38,000,000

13. Ask.fm – 37,000,000

14. Meet Me – 15,500,000

15. Classmates – 15,000,000

Advantages, Disadvantages and Risks

We use social media as a way of getting our message across to our chosen audience and we will do it with whatever means we have at hand. The most commonly used platforms for social media marketing are Facebook and Twitter, closely followed by Instagram, YouTube, Vimeo, Reddit and many others.

Social media does have a number of advantages and disadvantages, as well as some inherent risks and many businesses really do struggle to learn how to use this kind of marketing to the best advantage.

Advantages of Using Social Media

The biggest advantage to using social media for marketing purposes is cost. Most social media sites are free to join, to create a profile and to post information. The advantage to being able to reach your targeted audience for little to no cost should appeal to everyone and the audience you reach joins you of their own volition.

You can pay for advertising but the cost is little compared to the benefits that are reaped and the viral nature of social media means that, when one person reads your posts, they can spread it to their followers, who spread it to theirs, and so on. Information has the capacity to reach large swathes of people very quickly, sending your business multinational.

Another advantage is that you can truly find out what your customers think of you and your brand. Most people are quite happy to post a comment telling you what they think of your posts and they are quite happy to show you how happy they are by sharing.

Disadvantages of Using Social Media

Looking after a social media account can take a good deal of time and if you have more than one, it becomes very time consuming. You should hire someone who knows all about social media marketing to manage your accounts for you and be in a constant lookout for new angles to use, to keep relevant information reposted for as long as needs be and to post new stuff when the time is right.

The Biggest Risk of Using Social Media

There are a number of risks to using social media for marketing, one of which we addressed above. If you don't have someone on hand to check your accounts daily, disgruntled customers who don't receive a response to their complaint or request, can easily make life very difficult for you. Bad news travels much quicker

Social Media Marketing

than good and your business can suffer irreparable damage. Keeping on top of things is vital if you want your business to succeed at its social media marketing strategy.

Chapter 2

Why Social Media Marketing?

Who Can Benefit from a Social Media Strategy?

1. A large corporation with an established business who are just entering the social media marketing world

2. A small brick and mortar business such as a restaurant, hair salon, bakery, hotel etc.

3. An online business that is entirely based on social media

4. Individuals offering their services online such as freelance writers, illustrators, web designers, software developers, lawyers, doctors etc.

5. Independent artists such as musicians, authors, painters, filmmakers etc.

6. Individuals who want to build passive income streams through blogging, affiliate marketing, selling products on Amazon etc.

7. Any organizations such as charities, not-for-profit organizations, local libraries, government organizations etc.

Basically, anybody and everybody can use social media marketing to achieve their goals, be it selling products and services, spreading awareness about a cause, providing customer support or information about the company.

The Real Benefits of Social Media Marketing

To some business owners, social media marketing is the next big thing in marketing. To others it's just a fad that may be powerful but won't last long. As such, it must be used to its full advantage while we have it. Others see it as just another word that has no real advantage and takes way too long to learn. The fact is that social media has changed the world of marketing and it is here to stay.

Social media appeared almost overnight and has developed itself a bit of a reputation for being something of a passing interest and, because of that, cannot possibly be profitable. The statistics tell another story. In 2014, 92% of marketers claimed that the use of social media was vital to the success of their business and 80% of those said that their efforts in social media marketing increased traffic to their websites significantly. Right now, 97% of all marketers use social media but 85% don't know which tools to use for the best results.

Social Media Marketing

This just shows that there is a huge potential for social media to significantly increase sales but that there is a real lack of understanding on how best to use social media to get these results. The following are just some of the ways in which social media can help push your business into the limelight:

1. Increase in Brand Recognition

Any time you get the opportunity to increase your visibility and make people more aware of your content, you should grab it with both hands. Social media networks are new channels for your content and for your voice and this is important because it does two things – it makes you more accessible and more visible to new customers and makes existing customers recognize you easier and you become more familiar to them.

For example, someone who uses Twitter on a frequent basis may hear for the first time about your business through his Twitter feed. Then when he sees your name on another site or in the real world, he can recognize your brand from your Twitter profile. Or a customer who might otherwise be somewhat apathetic could become better acquainted with you and your brand after seeing your name pop up on several major social media sites.

2. Better Brand Loyalty

Research has shown that businesses that engage with customers on social media channels can expect to be rewarded with higher loyalty. Businesses should take full and frank advantage of the tools that social media marketing offers when it comes down to building a connection with their audience and helping them to become loyal to your particular brand. Further research shows, to back that up, that 53% of Americans who follow specific brands via social media are more likely to be loyal to those brands than they are to any other.

People want to connect with brands that seem more human. They don't like large cold corporations who maintain a condescending relationship with their customers. Instead they might prefer a small business which takes the time to do some real communication with its customers. For the first time, the small business owner has a level playing field with large multinational corporations through social media. And if done right, small businesses might even have a distinct advantage.

3. Better Conversion Opportunities

Every time you post on one or more of the social media platforms, you are giving potential customers the opportunity to convert to paying customers. When you build up a following on these sites, you are able to access new customers, look after old customers and interact with everyone on a more personal level. Every post, photos, video or comment that you put on your social network is giving people a chance to react and each reaction has the potential to lead to a visit to your website and a future conversion. Of course, not every person who interacts with your brand on social media will convert but every positive interaction increases the chances that a positive conversion will happen.

4. Higher Conversion Rates

Social media marketing has a positive effect on conversion rates in several ways. The most significant and important is one called the humanization element – brands become more humanized through social media interaction and can act just like other people do. This is important because people prefer to deal with people, rather than a faceless web contact form or a computer. Recent studies show that social media provides a higher lead-to rate than traditional outbound marketing by 100% and having more followers leads to a higher element of trust being placed on your brand, as well as credibility. The conversion rates for social media marketing are higher than any other form of traditional marketing out there.

5. Higher Brand Authority

Regular customer interaction through social media sites shows good faith to outside customers. When other people read a compliment or a "brag" from a person about the services or product they received, they suddenly sit up and start to take notice. And the more people you have on social media that are talking about your brand, the more value that brand will have to new users. In addition to that, if you can have real interaction with some of the major influencers on social media sites then your visibility and authority will go through the roof.

6. An Increase in Inbound Traffic

If you don't use social media then your inbound traffic is going to be severely limited to those who already know your brand and to those who accidentally land upon your site while searching a specific keyword. Every account you sign up to on a social media site unlocks the door to another path leading back to you and every piece of content you post on those sites is another feather in your visibility cap. The better the content you post, the more traffic you will generate and that leads to more leads and more possible conversions.

7. Lower Costs for Marketing

According to recent research, 84% of marketers have found that just 6 hours work a week on social media was sufficient to increase their traffic. 6 hours is little compared to the size of the social media outlets and, by investing just one hour per day, you too can reap significant rewards. Social media marketing is mostly free but even the paid advertising is not expensive. Start small and you won't need to worry yourself about going over your budget. Once you get a bit more experienced and you start to get a feel for what your advertising is achieving, you can increase your budget and your conversions.

8. Best Returns on Investment

Social Media Marketing

Social media marketing gives the best ROI out of any other marketing plans. It's not easy to know the exact ROI in any marketing campaign but if you count all the benefits such as brand recognition and loyalty, along with the higher conversion rate and cheaper cost of marketing, you can begin to see the real ROI of social media marketing.

9. Much Better Rankings on the Search Engines

SEO, or Search Engine Optimization, is the fastest way to pick up the right traffic from the search engines. Unfortunately, to be successful at it, you have to be on top of the frequent rule changes. It used to be that you could update your blog on a regular basis and make sure your Meta tags and titles were optimized. Google and other large search engines now take social media into account when they are calculating your rank so having a strong presence on at least one site, if not more, sends a good signal to the search engines that you have a brand that is trustworthy, credible and legitimate. What that means is, if you want to rank for a specific set of keywords, it is almost mandatory that you have a strong social media presence.

10. A Better Customer Experience

At its core, social media is one of the largest and most open channels of communication there is. Every time you interact with a customer or a potential customer on social media, you have a big opportunity to demonstrate your level of customer service and to make your customer relationships better.

For example, if you get a customer complaint via Twitter, you can deal with it immediately, issue a public apology and put the problem right. This shows potential customers that you are on top of things and will do what you can to make things right. Alternatively, if a customer compliments you via a social media posting, you can thank them personally and publicly and recommend other products that you think they will like.

11. Improved Customer Insights

Social media gives you a huge opportunity to see exactly what your customers want and how they behave. An example of this is monitoring comments to see exactly what people think of your business. You can target your content creation lists to more specific audiences and you can see which type of content generates the most comments – and what they say. Conversions can more easily be measured on each social media channel and you will eventually find the perfect method by which to generate revenue for your company. You can create A/B split advertising campaigns and see which one works better. You can also target specific demographics and create advertising campaigns that are customized for them and get much better conversion rates.

Are You Convinced Yet?

Social Media Marketing

The above mentioned eleven benefits should have convinced you to sustain a long-term social media presence and marketing campaign. But, if I still haven't managed to convince you that you should get started right away, here are a few more points to consider:

1. Your Competition is ahead of You

You can bet the entire farm on that one. Your competition will already be on social media, which means, until you get yourself on there, potential customers are being poached away from you. Never let the competition get the edge over you while you sit by and let it happen. And if for some unknown reason, your competition hasn't yet set foot on social media, the gate is wide open for you to be the first through it and take full advantage of this amazing opportunity.

2. The Sooner You Start, the Sooner You Will See the Benefits

Social media is all about building up relationships and it grows as fast as your friends tell their friends, and so on. The sooner you get your presence known on social media, the sooner you can begin to grow that audience and work on your conversions. The longer you do it, the larger your following will be. Your marketing campaigns will become more effective and grow at an exponential rate.

3. The Potential Losses are Not Significant

In real terms, you really don't have anything to lose by getting on social media. It takes little time to create your profile and set up your page and then you can start posting. This is nothing compared to how long it can take you to get off and running with other traditional marketing methods. Jest a few hours a week, a couple of hundred dollars and the world is yours for the taking.

Chapter 3
Building Your Own Social Media Strategy

It is important to have a social media strategy in place before you begin your social media marketing campaign. We are all already on social media in one form or another. Except for those living under a rock for the past decade, most of us already have a personal Facebook, Twitter and Google+ account. So when individuals start thinking about social media marketing they feel that they just need to keep doing what they are already doing on such sites and just do more of it. At most people think about starting a blog and when after a few months, the numbers don't match their expectation, their blog stagnates and dies.

This is the wrong way of going about social media marketing. What you need is a social media strategy.

This strategy should be based on solid information about your market, a view of your goals and what you want to achieve, knowledge about how to best use the different social media tools, and an estimate of the amount of time and money you can invest in this permanently ongoing marketing campaign.

An Overview of a Social Media Marketing Strategy

Listen

It does not matter whether you want to do your marketing on the social web or not, you should always listen to what is being said online about your brand. You can learn a lot by listening to what people are saying about you, whether it is good or bad.

Target and Position

Once you start listening to what is being said about you, you should then decide which of the social media platforms you should utilize for your business. Work out where your best audience is and what they talk about, who the influencers are and what their passion points are. This is all so that you can communicate with your audience in a meaningful way.

Talk

Engage with your audience, start a dialogue with customers. Listen and respond to what people are saying, not just about you but also about other things. This isn't all about pushing sales and promoting your own products, it's about being seen as a human being. Be consistent and converse with people on a regular basis, that way you will gain the trust of your customers.

Protect

Protect your brand and address any negativity straight away. Be honest and be quick as well as being thoughtful about what you say. Resolving problems and apologizing can go an awful long way in the damage limitation stakes. In addition, assess if there has been any damage to your search rankings because of any negative feedback and, if you see negative links appear, address them quickly.

Measure

You have to understand how your strategy is working and to do that you need to measure the return that your investment is having. There are plenty of analytic tools that you can use; most social media sites provide their own. Be smart and measure everything.

Other Types of Digital Marketing Strategies

Social media marketing is rising to the top as the best way to market on the internet but there are other ways to market on the internet. These strategies have existed long before social media marketing came along and they developed as a result of marketers applying real world strategies to the digital world. All of these strategies are still used but it's safe to say that their day in the sun has long been over. Marketers are seeing diminishing returns from these strategies as well as other traditional marketing techniques because people have become immune to them. Social media marketing is the next level in the world of advertising and marketing.

Here are some of these strategies that you can still use but don't make them the cornerstone of your marketing strategy.

- **Banner Advertising.** Banners take up a certain space that is up for rent on a web page. You can imagine how old marketers translated billboards into digital banners. Of course banners on the web are much more powerful than billboards. Banner ads can be text, or they can have videos, audio or interactive buttons on them. This kind of advertising generally works on a click through basis – users click the banner and are taken to the website that is linked to it and that is paying for the advert. Real world billboards can't be clicked and you can never know how many people came to you after seeing your billboard. But with the advent of social media marketing, banners are seeing diminishing returns on investment. People just don't click on banners anymore.

- **Email Campaigns.** This involves sending emails to selected customers or to potential customers who have signed up to your email list. Sometimes these mails will be newsletters, other times they will include promotions or discounts. Sometimes advertisers will cold email you with an offer even though you didn't sign up for it. This is the evolution of the real world mail marketing strategy and its considered spam in most parts of the world. If you build an email list through your blog and don't spam them, email campaigns can still be powerful. You should definitely consider having a newsletter to go with your blog.

- **Viral Marketing.** These are campaigns that are like word of mouth but online, where people spread the message to their own followers, who in turn do the same thing and so on. This is something that happens on its own if you focus on producing high quality content for your audience.

- **Link Building.** This strategy involves getting others to link to your blog or website in order to increase the number of inbound links so that search engines rank your website higher than your competition. When done correctly it can help your website reach the front page of search engines and brings loads of traffic to you. But some people tried to game the search engines by using the I-link-to-your-website-you-link-to-mine method. The search engines changed their algorithm so that if you were using such types of methods, your site got penalized instead.

Some other strategies that you can use on the internet are:

- Using your status updates to post a link or talk about a product or a service

- Retargeting: targeting those specific people who clicked on your banner ad once by installing a cookie on their browser so that no matter which site they visit, they see your banner ads.

- Creating pages or groups that are specifically to hold a contest, market a new product or raise awareness of your brand

- Offering apps that are cheap or maybe free, that you can use to build a list and then up-sell to them later

Understanding Online Network Users

There is a good chance you are already using some or all of the above tactics in your strategy. Just keep in mind that social networks are collections of people and of businesses that have opted to join the network so that they can gain new business and do not necessarily want to be bombarded with advertising.

Evaluate just how much promotional and advertising material you can make use of without seeming overbearing and selfish. Be aware of the type of advertising you are using as well. And don't just think about advertising alone. The crux of social media marketing is to understand that what people value are genuine interactions. The "social" part is just as, or even more important. Be human and be genuine and post content that doesn't directly sell your content but instead provides entertainment or engagement or edification for your customers. It is almost a Zen like state to achieve when you "sell without selling."

Be sure to check the terms and conditions of any social media site you use to make sure that you are not stepping outside their boundaries.

Targeted Advertising

Online social media sites are real hotbeds when it comes to advertising space and many businesses have been very quick to realize that these sites have a captive audience for targeted advertising. Be very careful in your considerations of which networks you use and the kind of message you want to get across, to make sure you get the best return on your investment.

Many of the social network sites offer several different options for advertising. These include pay per view, pay per click, classified ads, banner ads and flash ads.

Advertising can be targeted to specific demographics – age, gender, location, marital status, etc. and some social sites offer tools that you can use for research, which can give you some very valuable profile information. This helps you to make informed decisions on whether a site is working for you or against you.

Network Marketing Do's and Don'ts

If you are intending to use online social networks as part of your marketing strategy, you should be aware of a few do's and don'ts that you must comply with or risk being banned or losing business:

DO:

- Make sure you research your chosen network thoroughly before you go ahead and start advertising. Understand who uses it and what kind of marketing they may be open to.

- Develop a set of metrics that you can use to track your campaign and work out whether it is working or not.

- Make sure that you are fully aware of all the regulations and rules that apply to online marketing on that particular social network.

DON'T:

- Flood network users with spam; quality is far better than quantity and nobody likes a spammer.

- Sell or pass any personal details about your customers or any other business without their express permission first.

Building Your Social Media Strategy

Your social media strategy will constitute of:

- Your online presence
- A content strategy
- Social network presence
- Brand image

- Analytics and

- Content management

Let's talk about them one by one.

Online Presence

As mentioned in the previous chapter, the first thing you need is a place where you can send prospective customers. It can either be a website or a blog.

So what really is the difference between a website and a blog?

Well, a website is usually made of static content. When you build a website, it has static pages that contain content that you don't change too often. These can be pages like the home page, the about page, contact page, product portfolio page etc.

A blog on the other hand has dynamic content. You write blog posts and publish them regularly. A website can have a blog section along with other static pages. And blogs can have static pages as well. The static pages don't usually have a comment section while blog posts usually do allow readers to post comments.

Comments make a blog more of a social network than a standalone website. In fact social networks such a Twitter and Facebook are often called micro-blogging sites because you are posting your thoughts and interacting with readers in a way similar to blogging.

The distinction between a website and a blog can get confusing sometimes. The best way to define it is that a site that only has static pages and no regularly updated posts is definitely a website. The rest are either blogs, or websites with a blog section.

A static website is almost never a good idea. If you are a business or an organization you should have a website along with a blog section. If you are an individual with a small business then you can make do with a simple blog. But in almost all cases you should have a section where you publish regular content. Regular content helps you keep your audience engaged and you stay relevant to search engines. Static sites that haven't been updated for years slowly sink to the murky depths of the internet.

We'll talk about blogging in more detail in chapter 4.

Content Strategy

What type of content you will create on your blog depends on many factors. The biggest factor is your target audience. Ask yourself, where do your target audience hang out and what kind of content they seek?

For example, if you are an indie musician your target audience contains people who listen to music online. Here your product and content intersect as your music is both your content and your product. But you can create other content as well. Fans would like to know more about you and your creative process. They'd like to know about your experience in the indie music industry. They might also like it if you talk about other musicians and do reviews or feature interviews with other interesting musicians. You can share what type of gear you use and how you record music. They'd like to see videos of your performances. You can even do a virtual live show using Google Hangout or other such Webinar services. All this should figure into your content strategy.

As another example let's say that you have a small business that sells organic produce. Your target audience is the local community unless you also ship products to national and international buyers. Your community will consist of those who are interested in organic farming. This group's other concerns will be climate change, sustainable living etc. So you can form a content strategy where you offer advice on organic farming and living in an environmentally friendly way. You can talk about health and fitness as well. You can offer this content in the form of blog posts or videos or even pictures or infographics.

As you can see, it is difficult to come up with a set of standard rules for creating your own content strategy. It varies a lot depending on your product, your target audience and of course your ability to create the right type of content. But I hope you can also see that it is not hard to come up with a solid content strategy once you think about the following points:

- Who is my ideal customer?

- What are their interests?

- Where are they spending time online?

- How can I create valuable content for these ideal customers?

Right now you should just focus on providing as much value to this target audience as you can. Also remember that your content strategy will change over time and you can adapt it as you gain experience.

Two Types of Content

Social media expert Gary Vaynerchuk classifies social media content into two categories: the jab and the right hook. In boxing, a jab is a short straight punch that doesn't do much damage in one go but establishes the boxer's range and makes the opponent vary of getting too close. But when a boxer puts a lot of jabs together, they start adding up. A boxer can seriously hurt his opponent just by using jabs all night long. The right hook on the other hand is a big powerful punch that is meant to knockout the opponent. Good boxers know that the best strategy is to use a lot of jabs before throwing a right hook.

In terms of content, you should think of your jabs and right hooks. A content jab is any piece of content that entertains and engages your audience without trying to sell anything. A content right hook is that big sell that will be the center of your social media strategy. After all, you are doing all of this to sell something, be it your book, a course, an album, a product or a service. The important thing to note is that you shouldn't be throwing a lot of right hooks and very few jabs. High quality engaging jabs will make sure that when you do throw the rare right hook, it's more effective.

Make sure that whether you are creating a jab or a right hook, the quality of your content is always high. The internet is overloaded with content and marketers. What sets you apart from others is the level of your content's quality. But there is no point in going crazy after quality and not producing enough quantity. Best practice is to go for as high quantity as you can while maintaining high quality. It's neither 'quality over quantity' nor 'quantity over quality' but rather 'both quality and quantity.' That's what will make you a successful social media marketer.

Social Network Presence

Once you figure out a content strategy, you need to figure out how you are going to stay connected with the audience. There are hundreds of social networks to choose from and your choice has to depend on where your target audience is.

Here are a few tips to choose the right social networks for your social media marketing:

1. Don't start with too many social networks.

Most people have an account on all the popular social networks but it is very hard to manage all the accounts in the right way. What they do is that they create content on their blog and then share links to their content and products on every social network. But that isn't a very successful strategy because you are not forming real bonds with your audience anywhere. You end up just becoming an annoyance as you spam everyone with promotional content all the time.

2. Start with just one or two social networks.

Try to form real connections with a small group of people on that network. It's hard to produce high quality content specially designed to suit a particular social network. If you are an individual or small business owner who can't invest enough time and resources to produce quality content for all social networks then it's better to stick to just one or two networks. Do less but do it right.

3. Your content strategy will also be a factor in choosing your social network.

For example if you are going to make videos then you have to be present on either YouTube or Vimeo. If you are going to share pictures then you have to be present on Pinterest or Instagram.

4. For business to business (B2B) services Linkedin is a good social network to be active on.

Linkedin is also good for professional networking for freelancers.

5. Be present on at least one of the big three: Facebook, Twitter and Google+.

It is hard to ignore Facebook, which has over a billion people on it but there can be situations where it makes sense to not be present on Facebook, especially if you are not going to be able to provide value to your followers.

6. You start with a few social networks but as you grow your business you can hire social media managers or virtual assistants and be active on multiple networks.

Use the service called <u>Knowem.com</u> where you can automatically create an account on multiple social networks to book your brand name for the future. Even if you can't handle multiple social networks right now, make sure to book your brand name on as many sites as you can. It doesn't cost anything to create a profile so there is no reason to not do it.

Brand Image

It is important to have a clearly defined brand image before you get into social media marketing. Brand image includes, but is not limited to, a brand name, brand logo and a brand voice.

Whether you are an independent artist or a business, having a brand voice will help you create a better marketing strategy. Some brands have a comic or satirical voice while others are more classy and serious. It depends on your brand and the target audience but also on you. If you are an artist, then your own voice will be very close to your true brand voice. When you think about your brand voice, you can create a better content strategy and also form a cohesive image over all social networks.

A color palette and a design philosophy are also important for your brand image. The color palette will help with brand recognition. Don't you recognize the Coca

Social Media Marketing

Cola red immediately? That's a conscious brand image decision and if you create a unique palette that is used on your website and blog, your brand logo, and on your social networks, it will help create a unified and recognizable brand image.

The design philosophy will also work like the color palette and help in brand recognition. If your website and blog are minimally designed then you should maintain that design on the social networks as well. Use the same fonts wherever it is possible to do so.

Analytics

Your brand image will tie up all of your content and social networks together. The next step is to add analytics to your strategy. This is a great benefit of social media marketing over traditional forms of marketing because you can get a lot of data and use it to improve your future content and strategy.

There are various analytic tools that you can use to analyze your blog traffic and your social media outreach. Wordpress and other blogging platforms have their own analytics. You can use google analytics on your website as well. Facebook, Twitter, Google+ all let you analyze each and every one of your post in detail. You can find out how effective certain types of content are? Which time of day is best for posting content? What demographic is your biggest audience? You can use all this data to make sure that you are targeting your ideal customers through your content.

Analytics truly are the game changer when it comes to social media marketing versus traditional marketing. That's why analytics should form an important part of your social media strategy. If you are ignoring the analytical tools provided by these social networks then you are hurting your business.

Content Management

With all this content that you are going to create in your blog and on your social networks you also need tools for content management that will help you stay on top of everything. There are tools that can help you schedule social media posts and keep track of what you are posting in each social network. There are also tools for automating a lot of content posting and content aggregation. We'll talk about all this in more detail in chapter 8.

Before we get any deeper into all this, let's first go through the different forms of social media networks that you can use in your strategy. Once you understand how to use each one to its highest potential you will feel more confident forming your own social media strategy. I would recommend you to read all of the chapters from 3 to 7 even if you currently don't think you need to be present on certain social networks. Once you read all the chapters you'll be able to make a better decision about which social network to choose from.

Mobile Optimization

I just want to mention an important factor to keep in mind while building your social media strategy: mobile optimization. Smart phones have changed the way we live, the way we communicate, the way we get our information and also the way we seek entertainment. More and more people are now surfing the web on their phones. This means that you have to adapt your social media strategy to fit this new trend.

Your content has to be optimized in such a way that it can have an impact when viewed on a small phone screen as well as when viewed on a tablet or a laptop. In terms of your blog or website it means to have a responsive design which adapts to fit the screen size. This can be done easily by using a responsive theme. But there's more to mobile optimization than just responsive themes.

You have to adapt your way of thinking so that you are always thinking about how every piece of content will look on a mobile phone. For example, buying an ad on Facebook that shows up on the sidebar to the right is no longer as powerful as it used to be because a lot of people now use their phones to access Facebook and the right sidebar is not visible on their screens. A much better strategy for Facebook now is to buy sponsored posts and we'll talk about this in more detail in chapter 5.

But this example should help you understand how everything has to be adapted to suit the mobile experience now. And this is not just a fad that's going to go away very soon. As our phones get smarter and faster, more and more people will have only one device to do everything and that device is going to be the smart phone. So it only makes sense to adapt to this inevitable change as early as possible.

Part 2
Learning about Social Networks

Chapter 4

Blogging

We've already talked about how important a blog is for any business that is using social media for marketing. There is no doubt that you must have a blog. You can either get by with a simple blog based website or have a website designed for you and add a blog to that. There are a lot of services that will allow you to easily create a simple website using pre-made templates but I would recommend you to have a professional website designed by a web designer if you want to seem professional.

If you do not have the money to hire a web designer at this time, then a blog is the best solution for you. Designing a blog using pre-made themes and templates is much easier than designing a complete website. You can do it for completely free but if you are ready to spend just a little bit of money you can design a fairly professional looking blog with ease.

There are plenty of services that you can use to create your blog. Wordpress, Blogger and Tumblr being some of the biggest platforms.

Wordpress.com Vs Wordpress.org

Wordpress is the most commonly used blogging platform but you should know the difference between wordpress.com and wordpress.org.

Wordpress.com is a fully hosted blogging platform where you can put up your own blog. Basically this means that your blog will be hosted on wordpress' servers.

This has both advantages and disadvantages. For complete beginners, it is a great choice because it's simple and completely free. Wordpress will take care of backing up, updating and protecting your blog on their server. All functionality will come built in and preloaded. You can just sign up, choose a free theme you like and start blogging within a few hours.

The disadvantage is that it is like opening up a stall in someone else's shop. You don't own the property and so have much less control over it. If you are willing to spend a little bit of money you can buy a custom domain name and get a lot of high level functionality on wordpress.com as well. A custom domain like *www.yourblog.com* is much more professional than *www.yourblog.wordpress.com* that you would get for free with wordpress.com.

Wordpress.org on the other hand is a self hosted blogging platform. You can install it on your own servers and then build your blog on it. It is free to install but you'll have to pay for the server space to a hosting company. You will be responsible for security, backups, updating and adding all kinds of functionality, through plugins, to your website. This gives you far more options in terms of what kind of site you want to create but it is also a bit technical and more work than a simple blog. You can hire wordpress developers who can design a very professional blog and website all on the wordpress platform. If you have the technical knowledge or the time and desire to learn, you can master wordpress.org in a little while. It's not at all difficult if you are an analytical thinker. But if you don't have the time or are not willing to learn so much technical stuff, then wordpress.org can be a pain in the neck for you.

For beginners, I would recommend starting with a wordpress.com account. Pay for a custom domain and a premium theme and you can get a professional looking blog quickly, cheaply and easily.

Other Blogging Platforms

Blogger is owned by Google and is similar to wordpress.com as it is a fully hosted blogging platform. You can use custom domains in blogger as well, or go with the free *www.yourblog.blogspot.com* domain.

Tumblr is slightly different than blogger and wordpress. It is halfway between a blogging platform and a social network. In fact, after Yahoo bought Tumblr in 2013 for a whopping $1.1 billion, the young founder David Karp was heard calling Tumblr a social networking platform. Tumblr focuses on artistic visual content and GIFs or looping images. It is one of the few social networks which allow GIFs and you'll see a lot of them on Tumblr. It is best suited for pictures but it can also be used to create blogs with some stunning typography as well.

The community on Tumblr spends much more time on the network than other blogging platforms and that's why it's more like a social network. If your content suits Tumblr and you want to build your blog on it, make sure you are willing to spend enough time on the site to browse, repost and interact with other users.

Other blogging platforms include Typepad, Livejournal, Medium etc. There are hundreds of platforms to choose from but unless you have a very strong reason to go for some particular blogging platform, you should go for wordpress as it offers the most professional looking blogs which you can create with ease and at a low cost.

What to Blog About?

This is a question that bothers most people who have never blogged before. They feel that they are not good enough writers or that they just don't have enough ideas to write about. They feel that if they start blogging, after about a month they'll just run out of ideas. But in reality once you start blogging you might feel overwhelmed by the flood of ideas you want to write about.

Whether your blog is the main part of your website or just a small part of a bigger website, you should consider your audience before thinking about what to post on your blog. How can you provide value to your target audience? If you are an indie author maybe your audience would like to read about your writing rituals. Maybe you can share the journey of your upcoming novels. You can share chapters and get feedback from your readers.

If you are a small business of any kind, you can write about your industry, your own company, other companies in your industry etc. You can write articles about how your company does things in a better way than the rest of the industry. You can share customer reviews, pictures of your business, videos of happy customers etc. If the latest news stories have affected your business or your life you can write about that.

The sky is the limit when it comes to what you can blog about. It all depends on your creativity and imagination. The only thing you should keep in mind is, whether this content will provide value to your audience or not. If you are always aware of this basic tenet of blogging, you'll never go wrong.

Blogs are not as formal as an article in a newspaper or a magazine. You can get up close and personal with readers in a blog. You can use a more conversational tone and that is why blogs have become so popular. People now prefer to get their news from blogs which sound more human. So don't worry about being a good writer. If you can communicate well verbally then you can blog as well. And if the thought of writing still bothers you, why not create a video blog!

How Frequently Should You Blog?

This is the second question that new bloggers are worried about. The frequency can be anything from several articles a day for large multi-author blogs to just one article a month. The frequency depends on your business, your brand voice and how much time you can invest in blogging. The best frequency is to have 1 or 2 articles per week.

What is important is that you always stick to your frequency. You shouldn't be sporadic in your blogging. This means that you can't blog 5 posts in one week and then not blog for 3 weeks. This kind of inconsistent blogging portrays an image of an amateur blogger. If your blog is only for personal gratification then you can afford to be sporadic but if it is part of your social media strategy then you must be professional.

Editorial Calendar

This is where having an editorial calendar comes in handy. You should write blog posts in a text document, instead of directly in the content box provided on your blogging platform, and store it in a folder on your computer. This will help you plan your content better. You can create a buffer of articles that are ready to be published so that in case you get behind schedule, you still have articles to post and stick to your blogging frequency. It will also let you post better articles because you will create a gap between writing and editing which you can do while posting the article. Writing in a text editor will help you keep the spelling errors and typos to a minimum.

Ideally plan your editorial calendar for the coming month. Have ideas about the articles you are going to write and have the first few articles already written. Take the time to hone the article by going through several drafts before finally publishing. Spend some time thinking of good headlines for your articles. Find good pictures to go with your articles and deliver high quality articles. Remember to use copyright free pictures and mention the creator whenever possible.

Social Integration

If you use most fully hosted blogging platforms, they will come with preinstalled social integration plugins. You can have social sharing buttons at the bottom of your posts. You can also have the Facebook like button as a plugin. These buttons allow your readers to share your posts on their own social networks. This is where the power of social media marketing really comes into its own.

Imagine having just a 100 dedicated followers and all of them share your posts on their own social networks. Everyone has multiple followers on multiple social networks. This means that if you build a small but strong base of followers you can amplify your posts and reach a large number of people. And if you keep providing valuable content, you'll increase your followers steadily.

If you are using self hosted wordpress for blogging, you will have to choose social integration plugins and install them on your own but it is not as hard as it sounds as there are multiple plugins to choose from.

You can also automate sharing of your posts on your social networks. But when using this function you need to be careful because a simple generic link is not the best way to share content. A better way to share content is to do it manually and create interesting snippets about your post suited specifically for each social network. We'll talk about this in more detail in the next chapter.

Comments

An important part of blogging is interacting with your readers through comments. You should encourage your readers to leave comments and then spend some time interacting with these readers who actually take the time to comment on your blog.

Comments allow readers to form a strong bond of communication with the blogger. Even if you are a business and run a business oriented blog, you can still interact with the readers in the comment section. A lot of popular bloggers have removed comments from their blogs because after a while it gets literally impossible to reply to each and every comment. But if you are starting out, it always makes sense to have comments and use them to form close bonds with your readers.

Be honest and genuine in your replies. If you are a business you might have to use a more professional tone but it doesn't mean that you have to sound like a robot. Be human and express emotions. Don't be fake. This advice is important for comments on your blog as well as interacting with your audience on other social networks.

You should also be vigilant against spam in your comments. There are spammers who will comment on your blog with a link that they want to share. Their comment will be something generic like "I really love your blog" or "This is a wonderful article for anyone who's interested in this topic." If your comment section gathers a lot of spam, the real readers will be discouraged from reading your comment sections. Remember that comment sections often turn into discussion panels as readers reply to other readers' comments. It's a healthy environment for engaging with readers but that's why it's important to weed out spam comments.

You can do this by setting up comment moderation so that whenever a new comment comes in, it sits in a moderation queue. You have to manually accept or reject it before it shows up on your site. You can also set it up so that regular readers' comments don't end up in the moderation queue because you want regular readers to be able to see their comments immediately after posting them.

Guest Blogging

A good way to spread the word about your blog is by posting articles on other blogs. This is known as guest blogging. Find the leading blogs in your industry and see if they allow guest posts. Pitch articles that you think will provide immense value to the readers of that blog. This will help you reach your target audience and they'll get to know more about you through the author byline that goes with the blog post.

Guest blogging was the best way of building inbound links and increasing the rank of your blog on search engines. But this practice was misused to game the system and now you have to be careful about how your inbound links look. But if you do guest blogging sincerely there is no reason to worry. It still is a good way to get going especially when you are just beginning.

When you are new, it makes sense to actually save the best of your articles for guest blogging. If you post them in your own blog, no one will read them because your blog is new and has a limited readership. You want your best content to reach as many people as possible. And that can happen on the top blogs in your niche.

Before approaching bloggers for guest blogging, make sure that you have been following their blog for some time and know the type of articles they post, the style and tone of writing, and who their audience is. If you spend some time building a relationship with that blogger on social networks or by commenting on their blog, it will help your chances of being accepted for guest blogging.

Remember that reading blogs and commenting on popular blogs is the first step in guest blogging. Form real connections with popular bloggers and your blog will grow rapidly. You can also allow other bloggers to post guest posts on your blog. This will help you get good content for free and also increase your readership as the guest blogger will share that post to their social network as well.

SEO

Let's talk about another important topic that new bloggers feel scared of: Search Engine Optimization or SEO. Basically it means making your content friendly to search engine 'bots that scan your site for specific keywords. There is nothing wrong with this and the most basic techniques are simple. You just need to have the important keywords in the important places.

For example, if your article is about organic food then it will rank higher on search engines if the keyword "organic" features in the article's title, in the article's body, in the URL for the blog post, in the meta-description of the post etc. This is simple common sense. But certain SEO specialists try to take this approach too far. They try to come up with ways to game the search engines into ranking their posts higher than they deserve.

There is a point where SEO crosses over from common sense to cheating and this is a line that you shouldn't try to cross. It is called as White Hat SEO when you stay within the rules and Black Hat SEO when you try to game the system. Search engines are always updating their search algorithms that punish cheap SEO tricks and reward genuine quality content. So don't worry too much about SEO and just remember to use the right keywords in the right places. That's al the SEO you need. In wordpress you can install SEO plugins that remind you to add keywords in the right places.

The basic principles to remember for good SEO are:

- Your most important keyword should be a part of the post's title.

- Your URL should also have your keywords.

- Your post's meta-description should have these keywords. But don't just stuff the meta-description with keywords. It should make sense to a human and have only the necessary keywords.

- Your blog post body should have the keywords as well. This is common sense but don't try to force keywords where they don't belong. If you write a good article, it will naturally contain the keywords enough times.

- When putting pictures in your blog, make sure to use the alt-description section to define what the picture is about. Use your keywords here as well.

- Tag your post with the relevant keywords but don't use too many tags.

- Add the post to a relevant category on your blog.

These are basic principles of SEO and anything more advanced than this is not necessary but only optional. It also might be flirting with the line between White hat and Black hat SEO.

6 Social Media Practices that will Boost SEO

Both social media marketing and SEO are tightly woven together. They are both inbound strategies that focus on building up your identity in a way that attracts visitors to you naturally. Social media relies heavily on quality content and having a very visible and very strong brand presence, so any effort that you expend on increasing your SEO can easily double your reach on social media. Most of the top marketers will tell you that the reverse is true as well – the better your social media presence, the higher your search rankings.

Unfortunately, many marketers don't tell you just how you can influence your Google search rankings using social media. Instead of telling you how and why, they tend to write it off as a generality, which can leave social media marketers wondering if their social media strategies are actually as effective as they thought they would be. To fix this, I have come up with six social media practices that are proven to boost your SEO effectively:

Social Media Marketing

1. Increase your Numbers of Followers

Believe it or not, the total amount of your followers and social media connections has a real significant effect on your SEO rankings. A company that has 100 followers on Twitter is not going to get anywhere near the ranking that a mega-company with a million followers and a million Facebook likes is going to get. That said, there are a few stipulations to this. Google is fully able to detect whether your followers are genuine or not so this means buying 1 million likes on Facebook is not going to increase your rankings. In fact, the way that Google works now, it could even work against you.

It takes time to increase the number of followers you have but provided your efforts are consistent, it is very effective. Make sure your brand is presented in a unique manner and use the same voice on a daily basis to keep your users up to date. Post useful stuff – helpful hints, photos, videos, open inquiries and general discussions - and make sure that you follow up any comments and engage your users in a friendly but professional manner. Conversing with your customers is one of the key building blocks to keeping hold of a decent number of followers as these encourage others to return to the fold and help to build up your authority to gain new followers.

But beware about getting too lost in the numbers. There is no point in gaining followers only for the sake of having larger numbers to brag about to your friends. There is a "you scratch my back and I'll scratch yours" mentality on many social networks. People on Twitter specifically mention on their bio that if you follow them, they'll follow back. In this way a lot of people on Twitter have built up thousands of followers. You can see that these followers are not genuine by the fact that the person also follows thousands of people. If someone has 50,000 followers but they follow 51,000 people then that person is most probably guilty of adopting this strategy.

In this way you can inflate your numbers for sure but it's not going to have any meaningful effect on your SEO or your marketing ROI. Think about it, all these people are just following each other blindly without really being interested in their products. They can't possibly stay on top of tweets of 51,000 people. They never even see others' tweets and just go on tweeting their own right hooks. "Buy my book!" "Read my blog!" and on and on they go, shouting at the top of their voice without listening at all. This is exactly the kind of follower you should run away from. And run fast.

So while increasing your number of followers is important, don't get lost in the numbers. Hand curate a list of followers who really like your product and who communicate with you and listen to you when you speak.

2. Encourage External Inbound Links

Another way that social media is useful is that it encourages external websites to link to your website. The more diverse the external links you have, the better your authority in Google's eyes. Of course, there is a catch to this as always and that is

Social Media Marketing

that you must have high quality content that is authoritative to start with. Otherwise, there will be nothing there to attract those links.

In this way, social media simply serves as a kind of broadcasting channel. Assuming that your content is original and is deemed useful, it is going to be used as some kind of bait. The fishing poles are your social media channels, putting the bait right where it can be seen by everyone. Make sure you use hashtags for the initial round and don't be too shy of bringing your own content into discussions and existing threads. When done in moderation and with the sincere desire to help others, this will improve your reputation as a leader in your market and it will also maximize the number of sources available for external linking.

3. Making Sure Your Posts are Optimized for Searches

This relies quite heavily on existing content as well as new but it does open up a secondary channel for searching. As well as Knowledge Graphs and news articles, Google favors social media updates that are popular in its top search rankings. It is a good position, albeit only temporary, that you can get to by making sure all your posts are fully optimized.

To do that, you need a very strong anchor for your post. It can be anything – a video, an infographic, a link to a long article that is full of information and detail. Whatever you choose, it is going to be the foundation and you must make sure that your title is accurate and descriptive.

Next, when you post it, make sure that the foundation is framed with text that is fully optimized for a specific search type. Fore example, you have written a highly informative and detailed article on how to make the best oatmeal cookies. Consider framing it with something along the lines of "Have you ever wondered how to make a truly delicious oatmeal cookie?" Use seasonal keywords if you like, depending on the time of the year and that will maximize your chances of being found in the search results.

4. Influence Social Sharing

Social sharing plays quite a big part in the authority of your brand, almost as much as external linking does. To any search engine, if there is any indication that there is an external source that is validating your brand, provided that source can be verified, it is grounds for raising the profile of your domain authority. So, get ten people to share your post on Facebook, that's good. But get 1000 to share that same post and that's much better. Things that count towards increased authority are Likes, Retweets, Shares, Favorites, and replies.

The best way for you to encourage people to share your content is to create high quality content and offer them something in return. You could hold a prize draw for an expensive prize or you could hold interactive surveys, which ask people to like your post if they are in agreement with your opinion. The very best part about all of this is that this is a self-perpetuating circle. The more your content is shared, the more flowers you get, and the more followers you have, the more times your content will be shared, and so on.

5. Optimize Your Posts Locally

Social media offers you an opportunity to become fully engaged in your local community and you can do this by sending out local-specific signals to the major search engines. There are several ways you can do this but the easiest ways are to post updates whenever your company gets involved in events and by interacting with other establishments and local brands via social media.

The first way is easy – whenever you attend a show, a festival, any local event, take some photos and post them on social media. Invite people to comment on your post as well because this will reinforce the fact that you are participating in your local community and this will make you more visible when it comes to searches.

The second way takes a bit more. Carry out searches for local business and engage with them on a regular basis. Share posts, talk to each other, get involved in each other's discussions and post guest blog posts on each other's websites. Then share them to your social media sites.

6. Increase Your Brand Awareness

This might seem to be a little more like an advantage in terms of branding rather than in SEO but the SEO benefit is quite significant. If you can increase your social media reputation, by increasing your engagement and your high quality content, it will lead to a more recognizable online brand presence. That increase in presence will lead to even more branded Google searches and the more of those you get, the higher your non-branded keywords get ranked. It is a very complicated relationship but it all starts with a strong branded presence on social media and it ends with a much greater visibility across the search board. There is no particular way that you can improve your authority except to give your audience quality.

For a large part, these 6 practices are the staple elements of any successful campaign that combines both social media and SEO. Like most SEO principles, it all comes down to one – if you want to rank high in Google, you must give your users a quality experience. Understanding how social media and SEO affect one another is vital if you want to manage your campaign better and you want to ultimately give your audience a much better experience, as well as opening up the door wide enough for potential new customers to see your brand.

Capturing Emails

One important task for your blog will be to help you build an email list of subscribers. This email list will be very important for your social media

Social Media Marketing

marketing as it will contain the most hardcore fans of your brand. You can provide special offers to these highly targeted people in your emails. You can also use emails to send out a monthly or weekly newsletter that helps subscribers feel part of an inner circle. When this tribe mentality is activated, people will be happy to share your posts, buy your products and celebrate in your success.

It is easy to create a sign up form on your blog, no matter which platform you are using. Use an email list management service such as Aweber or Mailchimp to manage your list.

It can be a good idea to provide something for free in exchange of the reader's email. This is sometimes called a "bait" but think of it as a gift you are giving to potential readers to make a good first impression on them. This can be a free pdf report or an ebook related to your industry, it can be one of your products for free such as an album for a musician or an ebook for a writer, or it can even be discount coupons for your products.

If you send out newsletters, remember the most important rule of social media marketing; provide a lot of value to your readers. Your newsletters can't contain only promotional content all the time. It has to be meaningful for people to stay subscribed otherwise they'll sign up to get the free gift and then soon unsubscribe.

The last point I want to make is to not be too obsessive about getting your blog to be perfect as blogging is an ongoing process. The more you do it the more you'll learn and slowly your blog will get better.

Before we go into more detail about your social media strategy and how to execute it, let's talk about the most important social networks so that you have a good idea about which ones to use and how to make the most of them.

Chapter 5
Facebook

Facebook is the biggest and most powerful social network out there. It is the big daddy of social networks and a complete book can be written about ways to utilize Facebook for marketing, and in fact there are a lot of books just like that but since this is a book covering the overall basic strategy for social media marketing, I'll try to keep this section about Facebook as short as possible.

There are over 1.49 billion monthly active users on Facebook. 72% of all adults that are online, in one form or another, visit Facebook at least once a month. The average time spent per user per day on Facebook is 21 minutes. All this means that there are a lot of people from all over the world on Facebook and they spend a lot of time on Facebook. This makes it *the* place to be if you are a social media marketer. Unless you have a concrete reason not to be on Facebook, you should be on Facebook.

You can do a lot on Facebook. You can share any type of posts, just words, pictures, videos, check-ins, links to other social networks, links to other online content etc. You can also create groups and fan pages to engage with your target audience. You can use Facebook advertising, sponsored posts and insights to create highly targeted advertising. You can create events to rally people around a real world or virtual event, such as an online sale or a webinar etc. You can also use Facebook to keep track of your competition.

Profiles Vs Pages

If you are an individual who wants to use Facebook for social media marketing, it can get a little confusing whether to use a profile or a page.

A profile is basically your personal identity on Facebook. Every individual can have only one profile. You can't use your profile 'primarily' for commercial purposes. This means that if you are an author and you share a lot of links to the Amazon page of your books, you can get into trouble for using a profile for business purposes. If a user reports your profile, Facebook can look into it and may even delete your profile.

Facebook wants all businesses, whether big companies or individuals, to use the business page feature. When Facebook Pages started out, they were called fan pages, some call them business pages, band pages etc. but they are all basically pages. There are 6 classifications under pages which cover almost all social media marketers:

- Local business or place

- Company, organization or institution

- Brand or product

- Artist, band or public figure

- Entertainment

- Cause or community

If you are using Facebook only for personal use to stay in touch with friends then you just need a profile but if you are going to use it for social media marketing in any form then you need a page. Of course, you can have both as well.

Pages Vs Groups

To confuse things further Facebook also has a feature called groups. Pages are basically profiles for business accounts whereas groups are more like a forum or a community.

In a profile you can have friends and followers. In a page you can only have followers and people become your followers simply by liking your page. In a group people can become members. They can request to join a group and a group moderator accepts or rejects their request.

In a profile there is one on one communication between individuals. On a page there is one on one communication between businesses and customers. In a group there is many on many communication between the members of the group.

Which One to Choose?

As I mentioned earlier, if you want to use social media marketing tools you need to go for a page. It offers a lot of advertising tools and insights into how people are interacting with your page and also how your advertising campaigns are going. Pages also allow you to schedule posts whereas profiles don't allow that. You get a dedicated domain such as *www.facebook.com/yourpage* which helps you to direct traffic to your page from outside Facebook. Facebook has created all this functionality to make sure that all businesses use pages and you should make use of that.

In order to start a page you will need to have a profile. Whether you use it for personal use or not is up to you. You can create multiple pages for different businesses or different parts of your business. The only reason to start a group is if you want to build a community around a topic or interest. All three can be used to enhance your social media presence.

Facebook Ads

As a social media marketer on Facebook you need to master the various ad formats that you can use. Unfortunately, Facebook's ads are notorious for being extremely confusing. There are just too many options to choose from, too many ways to create ads and too much information to keep in mind to ensure that your ads give the highest ROI possible. But don't worry, I'm going to try and introduce you to the world of Facebook Ads in as simple words as possible.

First let's begin by how content is shared on Facebook. There are almost 1.5 billion people on Facebook and all of them are constantly creating content sharing status updates, photos, videos, links and liking and sharing other people's content. This means that an average user of Facebook will have 1500 new items on their news feed every time they log in to their account.

In order to not overwhelm the user, Facebook has come up with an algorithm which tries to ensure that only the most relevant content is shown to the user. This content is hand picked for every user based on theirs past behavior. Well in reality the algorithm is much more complex and it used thousands of factors to rank each piece of new content in the news feed and shows only that which is most relevant to that user.

This means that the organic reach of a post, or the number of people you can reach without having to pay for it, can be as low as 2.5%! That means that only 2.5% of your fans will see your posts. The only way to get more people to see your posts is to pay for them in the form of Facebook Ads.

Some people say that Facebook has deliberately reduced the organic reach of posts in order to force people to pay for reaching their audience. Facebook maintains that it is just trying to provide the best experience to its users and also to the businesses that choose to advertise on Facebook.

There are things you can do to increase your organic reach as well. Like post high quality content that's engaging and entertaining. Post at the right time. Ask your fans to not just like your page but subscribe to your notifications so that they never miss any of your posts. Set up a deal with other pages in your niche to share each other's content. Set up targeting for your unpaid organic post. Share links to your Facebook post on other social networks. But all these steps will not help you as much as investing money in Facebook Ads can.

Here are the different types of ads based on what objective you have:

1. **Boost Post**. To increase the number of people who see your post. You can boost posts to your fans and their friends or to a targeted audience.

Social Media Marketing

2. **Promote Page**. To get people to like your page and increase the number of fans of your page.

3. **Promote Website**. To get traffic from your Facebook page to your website.

4. **Website Conversions**. To get traffic from your Facebook page to your website and then get them to do some action there. Like buying your product or signing up to your newsletter.

5. **App Ads**. To get people to install your app on their phone.

6. **Offer Claims**. To give people an offer such as a discount on your product.

7. **Local Awareness**. To target people in your locality. A good option for a brick and mortar business to get more people to visit your business.

8. **Event Responses**. To invite participants to your events. Maybe virtual or real world event.

9. **Video Views**. To get people to watch your promotional video.

10. **Carousel Ads**. To display several products in one ad with a photo carousel.

11. **Dark Posts**. To create a post that is used as an ad for a targeted audience but isn't shown to your fans on their news feed or on your timeline.

As you can see there are many options to choose from. On top of this there are several ways to create an ad. For example you can boost a post directly from your timeline or go to your Ads manager and create a promoted post.

When you start creating an ad you get to choose many options to make it most effective. The most powerful option is to choose a target audience. You can go really deep into it and target a very particular set of people. To get a better understanding of who you should target, you can look at your insights and see the current audience that you have.

You can also set your maximum budget, the duration of your campaign, your goals, the type of your bid, the message, the headline, the visuals etc. You can choose where the ad appears on Facebook; desktop news feed, mobile news feed or right sidebar. Some types of ads are only available in one or two locations. It is better to go for news feed ads especially on mobile because the sidebar isn't even visible on the mobile screen and as mentioned earlier, more and more people are using their phones to surf the internet. But also beware to not create out and out right hook ads all the time for the news feed because people will report it as spam if you do it too much. Ads that sell out and out are best suited for the sidebar. The news feed is a good place to advertise your content jabs that are social in nature and not trying to obviously sell anything.

The boost post option has the advantage of pre testing your ads. Just promote the posts that are already seeing some good engagement. This way you'll be sure to get a good ROI on your money.

Success Tips for Facebook

Engagement is king. When you post something on Facebook and your fans like it and share it and comment it, this shows to Facebook that you have created some interesting and engaging content. So Facebook will show your post on more people's news feeds. They'll show it to more of your fans and also to friends of your fans who they think will like your post.

If you can create such type of content you can quickly build up on the positive feedback cycle that can result from this. Your fans like your post and more people get to see your posts. You gain more fans and so you get even more engagement on your future posts which makes your content more valuable for Facebook. When you decide to boost a post or create other advertisements, Facebook will offer you better rates and show your ad to more people so you'll get better ROI.

This is the best way to succeed on Facebook. Create great content.

Use Groups to drive engagement. Create a group for your hardcore fans. Keep it invitation only so to maintain exclusivity. Make your biggest fans administrators for your groups. This will help to make them more loyal to your brand and feel as if they are part of it. It will also help you manage the group without having to spend too much time on it. But the most important benefit of creating a fan group is that you can drive engagement through it. Whenever you post something on Facebook, also share it with the group members and ask them to share it with their friends.

You can also drive engagement by sharing your post on other social networks although if you do too much of this, the other social networks will consider you to be a spammer. It is important to create native content for every social network. You can instead ask your email subscribers to engage with your Facebook posts. But do this too often and they'll think you are a spammer.

Choose the right classification for you page because Facebook lets you enter specific information for each category that will make your page more visible.

Use a good page icon and a good header image to make your page appealing. Your logo will make a good icon for your page if you are a business. If you are an individual use a professional portfolio picture. A well designed header image can capture attention and tell the entire story about your brand with a few words and a picture.

You can even have a call to action on your header. Or you can remind people to enable notifications for your page so that they don't miss any of your content. You can also promote new products in your header images. For example, writer's can use header images that have their upcoming books on it. Find creative ways of using your headers and change it once in a while to keep your page looking fresh.

Add valuable content to your page. You can highlight important content to separate it from the rest. The content should be engaging, entertaining or educating to capture the interest of the viewers. Use all types of contents and don't stick to just one type. Use pictures and text and videos and links.

When it was revealed that Facebook news feed algorithm was giving preference to pictures a lot of people starting uploading their textual content as a picture. But such attempts at gaming the system don't work for long as soon Facebook changed its algorithm. Now they say that native videos are rated higher in the algorithm but this doesn't mean you create a text based video for your textual content.

Pictures are very popular on Facebook. Use high quality images that are interesting and captivating. Add text to the pictures to make them more likeable and shareable. But don't turn your text posts into inforgraphics that barely qualify as pictures. Also if you are going to turn your post into an ad you need to have less than 20% text on your pictures.

You can create your own pictures or get copyright free pictures from various sources on the internet. You can also buy stock pictures from sites such as Shutterstock. You can also share interesting pictures that you find on Facebook on your own page.

Facebook has introduced 15 second micro-videos to compete with Twitter's Vine. You can upload links to videos on YouTube and Vimeo as well but Facebook gives preference to videos that are uploaded directly on Facebook. The user can view the video directly from their news feed without getting redirected to another site. The autoplay function means that the video is already running and the user hits the play button just to unmute the video. And as mentioned earlier, Facebook is currently giving preference to native videos on the news feed.

When using written content on Facebook make it conversational. Ask questions and encourage people to take some action. It can be to like, share, click on a link, or to reply to the update. Twitter only allows 140 characters so people use Facebook for longer updates. But it shouldn't be too long. If you have a lot to say then post it on your blog.

When sharing links, don't add the link to the description as well. This negatively affects how the new news feed algorithm chooses to show your posts on the feeds of your fans. When you are linking to your own blog post, make sure you have a good picture associated with that post as Facebook will extract the picture and description of the post when you link to it.

When mentioning another Facebook user or page, use @name to include them in the conversation.

Schedule your posts to publish during the after-work hours and on weekends in the region of your target audience. Stats show that engagement with posts published at these times is higher than normal. Posts published during lunch breaks also get high engagement. If you have an international audience you might want to schedule posts at different times of the day to reach people all around the world.

Use Facebook ads intelligently. Target the right audience and create an engaging ad. Try out different ideas to see which one works the best. There's a lot of value to be had from learning to use Facebook ads in the right way.

Once you start getting engagement from your fans, **reply to their messages promptly**. Ideally it should be within a few hours. In a later chapter we'll talk about how you can hire a virtual assistant to do all these chores for you.

Use hashtags with care. Hashtags are mostly popular on Twitter and Instagram but they've made their way on to other social networks such as Facebook and Google+ as well. How you use hashtags depends on the social network and Facebook users don't like to see a lot of hashtags. Don't use more than one or two. The surprising thing is that Instagram, which is now owned by Facebook, prefers as many hashtags as you can use. So make sure you are tagging your posts according to the network you are posting on.

The most important tip as always is to not spam. Create valuable content that your fans will enjoy. Don't try to push promotional content down their throats. Be human and be genuine. Let your real personality, or your brand's voice shine through. Create 80% social jabs and only 20% promotional right hooks.

5 Common Social Media Mistakes on Facebook

Facebook marketing is a relatively new discipline for a large number of companies but it represents a fantastic opportunity as well as a significant challenge. Any marketing that you do via social media, including Facebook, requires you to change the way you think about your marketing campaigns. Traditional marketing is usually a one-way street but Facebook marketing is a definite two-way street, with active conversations between you and your community. Like other forms of social media marketing, Facebook marketing is known as "dialogue marketing".

Social Media Marketing

When you start your Facebook marketing campaign, mistakes can and do happen very easily. Don't worry though – the following are five of the most common Facebook marketing mistakes that companies make and learning what they are and how to avoid them by adopting good habits on Facebook will help you to boost your presence and your brand loyalty.

Mistake #1: Violating Facebook Pages Terms

Do not ever allow your social media campaign to violate Facebook Pages Terms. Social media promotions are highly valuable tools in helping a business to increase awareness and brand loyalty online. However, many companies, when they run a promotion, make one big mistake in violating the promotion guidelines that Facebook lays down. These are the same terms that you agreed to when you created your company page. When you create your page, you tick a box to say that you will not place any competitions on it and that you will not use any of the features or the functionality of Facebook as a way of promoting registration to your promotion or as a way of people entering your promotion. What this means in real terms is that you cannot post something that asks people to like the post for an entry into a draw or competition. Facebook has strict rules that third party apps must be used when you want to run competitions or promotions and that includes contests and sweepstakes.

Mistake #2: Using Monologue Marketing Instead of Dialogue

Never engage in monologue marketing because Facebook is all about dialogue marketing. The reason it is called social media is that you are socializing with your community. Your Facebook page isn't just another website. It isn't just for promoting your products, or giving details on new products or pricing. A good Facebook marketing campaign engages people in lively discussions; you spark off a dialogue between you and other people, be it through serious or lighthearted discussions or posts.

If someone posts a question on your Facebook page, make sure you answer it and do it quickly as well. Show your gratitude for any comments that people leave, make it look like you care for your audience and are keeping them gainfully engaged in a dialogue. Once you have increased your community, make sure you keep a track of all the conversations as and when they happen.

Mistake #3: Posting a Load of Rubbish

There are a lot of companies who consistently fill their Facebook pages with information about their product, pricing and links. Most of the time, these posts will not generate any kind of discussion or activity. While it's ok to post this kind of stuff every now and then, it's not OK to do it every day. People use Facebook as a means of social engagements, to talk to one another so keep your posts relevant, engaging and free of rubbish.

Post photos of your business, perhaps some behind the scenes images. Add in a bit of personal content, stuff that is entertaining. Use a few calls to action to get people to respond and ask questions. If your sales-focused posts are going to generate any traffic, your Facebook page has to be entertaining, quality and have plenty of variety in it.

Do not feel obliged to maintain a very high posting frequency. Unless you are a news website that has a lot of new content to share everyday, you should share about 1-2 times a week. That's the ideal amount for most social media marketers. Facebook is overloaded with content and what they are looking for now is great quality content. If you take the time to create excellent quality, then even one post per week will show great results. In fact, consider every post as an advertisement campaign, whether you decide to boost it or not. Spend that much time creating it and only them post it on Facebook.

Mistake #4: Not Measuring the Success of Your Campaigns Correctly

This is key to any marketing campaign, not just Facebook. Count your fans, your likes, your followers, whatever you call your community members. These are the people who are responsible for your success and they can break you as easily as they can make you. Track how many people are following you to see how well your marketing campaign is doing. There are a number of methods you can use, including:

- Seeing how many active followers you have on your page

- Check to see how quickly you respond to queries from those followers and whether you are responding to all messages or just some

- See which posts get the most likes and dislikes

- How many people actually see your posts?

- Check to see what is happening at a time when you gain new followers and, equally importantly, when you lose them

- How much has your website traffic increased because of your presence and activity on Facebook?

- Are your followers just visiting your website or are they converting to sales?

All of these can be used as a measure of how successful your campaign is. Using Facebook's analytical tools or insights is very important to create a really strong marketing campaign on Facebook.

Mistake #5: Not Having a Proper Facebook Marketing Strategy

Every company should know that, to be successful they need to have a strong presence on Facebook and they should hire themselves a marketing manager to help them manage it. Believe it or not, there are an awful lot of companies who do not have any kind of strategy and are just using adhoc campaigns. It is important

Social Media Marketing

that you have a set of goals for your Facebook marketing strategy and if you are not sure what those goals should be, you should start by looking at your whole marketing strategy.

Think of Facebook as an offshoot of the main marketing strategy. Set goals that relate to Facebook, that align with your main business goals and come up with strategies and tactics that are designed to drive your presence on Facebook. It isn't complicated, more time consuming yes, but once you have it right, your campaign will practically run itself.

So, there you have the top five mistakes made by companies who use Facebook, Make sure your company isn't making them too!

Chapter 6
Twitter

Twitter is the second biggest social network after Facebook. It has over a billion registered users and there are about 304 million monthly active users. Twitter has become the number one source for news and you can hear about any world event just seconds after it happens.

Twitter is different from most other social networks. This is mostly because of the 140 character limit on tweets. This limit was originally in place because Twitter began as a service that allowed you to tweet from your phone through SMS messages. So in a way Twitter brought social media to phones before phones became smart and could surf the web.

Communications on Twitter are short and fast. The live feed on your home page never stops. If you are not on Twitter while someone tweets something, you will most probably never see it. This adds to the uniqueness of this platform. As you read above, Facebook uses an algorithm to prevent exactly this from happening. But Twitter embraces this chaotic speed at which information is shared. Now, Twitter has come out with a "while you were away..." feature. So when you log on to your account, Twitter tries to show you old tweets from accounts that it considers are important to you. But once you've seen these tweets you can close this section and get back to the current feed.

It is important to note that like a lot of other social networks, Twitter is changing all the time. There are talks about lifting the 140 character limit from certain tweets. But whatever changes may come, hopefully they'll stay true to the unique essence of Twitter that makes it special.

You can see that Twitter is special from the way people use it. The same people who won't accept a stranger's friend request on Facebook, are more than happy to follow strangers on Twitter. Facebook is for your existing and old friends but Twitter is for making new friends. This makes it a very promising platform for social media marketers. You can build a considerable following with much more ease than other social networks and if your tweets are retweeted multiple times you can get widespread exposure and reach potential customers.

How People Use Twitter

It is important to understand how people use Twitter in order to come up with an effective strategy for this network. A lot of the normal everyday users of Twitter use it to make new friends, become part of communities around a certain niche or topic, follow celebrities and share news and opinions of their own.

Social Media Marketing

Then there are the celebrities and big brands that use Twitter to connect with fans. A lot of big and small businesses use Twitter as a fast way to handle customer complaints and feedback.

There are certain popular accounts that create interesting or funny content specifically for Twitter. Such accounts often tweet famous quotes or short and witty tweets related to world events. This is a great way to build up following but requires a lot of time and effort as you have to view Twitter not just as a social network but as a micro blogging platform.

A lot of people on Twitter are the wannabes. These are emerging writers, musicians, artists, who have been told that if you can build your Twitter following, you can become famous and be able to sell your art to a lot more people. The trend in this community is to follow each other back in order to boost each other's numbers. Some bios clearly mention that if you follow them, they will follow back. In this many people have build up tens of thousands of followers. But they also follow the same number of people.

Do not fall into this trap. Twitter is not just about numbers. Imagine what kind of exposure these people get to their tweets when all of their followers are just like them; on Twitter just to self promote. Everybody is busy pushing their products to those who are trying to push their own products and have no interest in others. It's madness! It is better to have just a few hundred followers, but those that actually read and respond to your tweets, than to have 100,000 followers who never read your tweets.

Finally there are a huge number of automated bots on Twitter. This is annoying to say the least. As soon as you tweet about a certain keyword, the bots will follow your account trying to get a follow back. But these types of followers are just as useless as the self promoters.

This information should help you to understand the Twitter user base better. You can then try to find genuine people interested in you or your product and build genuine relationships with them.

Twitter Cards

If you want to use Twitter for social media marketing you have to be familiar with Twitter cards. These are special ways of tweeting that are designed to get a certain type of engagement or response from the followers. Twitter cards can be a little overwhelming for those who are not technical minded because there is code involved in using them. But if you take some time to understand Twitter cards, you'll find that the technical part is easy to understand and implement. And the benefits you can receive by using these cards far outweigh the slight pain of understanding them.

Social Media Marketing

Twitter cards lets users create varied content in a world of 140 character texts and links. And they are absolutely free to use. This is what makes them powerful and also a must have in every social media marketer's arsenal. Let's discuss these cards in short here to get you going.

Summary Card

Summary cards contain a thumbnail image, a title and a description. They also contain account attribution and they link to an external page. These cards are great for sharing new content on your blog with your followers. If you share a simple link, it will be visible as text followed by an html link. That's not particularly appealing. But a summary card allows the user to get a glimpse of the page being shared with an image and a description.

Summary Card with Large Image

If your content has a beautiful picture as a centerpiece, or maybe an infographic that you'd like to share on Twitter you can use the summary card with large image. As the name suggests it's just a summary card but the image is much larger than a thumbnail. It takes up the entire width of the timeline and your title and description follows below. This is a great way of standing out in the Twitter feeds of your followers. But remember that twitter cards have the limitation that they don't come automatically expanded but rather with a "view summary" button at the bottom right corner of the tweet. If the user clicks on this link, only then does the card appear.

App Card

The app card is wonderful for those who want to promote an app to their Twitter followers. This card comes with details of the app along with an option to directly download the app on the users' phone. Since more and more people are using their smart phones to surf the web, it has become a great way to promote your app on social networks which users can download directly to their phones with a single click.

Player Card

The player card is to stream video/audio/or other media in your tweets. Other media might be GIFs or short vine videos. These cards allow users to view your videos or listen to your audio without having to leave Twitter. This is important because when people are using a social media site, they don't really want to leave it and go off on a tangent as that can be distracting.

Player cards require a little while to be approved and are based on the content of your media.

There used to be photo, gallery and product cards but these have been retired by Twitter. To use a card all you have to do is add a few lines of code in the meta section of your site's html file. This section has extra information about the webpage that does not effect how the page looks. You can get these lines of code from Twitter and easily copy paste them to your website's html page. If you can't access your site's html directly, like if you are using a blogging platform like wordpress, you can find a way to get around that limitation. Most platforms have built in tools to help you ad Twitter cards to your webpage.

Once the code is pasted you need to validate it using Twitter's validator tool. Once it has been approved there is nothing more to do. Once a card has been set up, it will show up on its own no matter who tweets your link. This is a great advantage of using twitter cards. For example, once you set up a summary card for your website's home page, whenever someone shares your home page with their own followers, their tweet will appear with a summary card.

You can use card analytics to measure how each card performs. Analytics are a major part of Twitter and you can even see analytics for each one of your tweets. But card analytics give you specific information about how each of your cards is performing.

Twitter Ads

The last thing you need to know about Twitter is about its ads services. Just like Facebook, you can spend money on Twitter to promote your content to targeted audiences. Using Twitter cards and Twitter ads you can create a powerful marketing campaign for your business. There are several type of campaigns you can create on Twitter.

Tweet Engagements

This type of ad will promote your tweets and bring it to a greater audience. A promoted tweet is specifically labeled as such at the bottom left corner. It is a great way to reach a bigger audience than your followers and you can earn new followers this way. You bid for certain actions such as retweets, favorites, replies etc. to drive engagement of your tweets. Each time that action is performed you have to pay a certain amount of money.

Website Clicks or Conversions

You can promote your website through this type of ads. You can use these ads along with summary cards to promote your website and direct traffic to the landing page of your product. By using a conversion pixel you can even choose to pay only when someone actually clicks on your call to action on your landing page. (A conversion pixel is just a piece of code that measure how many people actually click on the call to action and covert)

App Installs or App Re-engagements

This goes great with the app card. Get your app in front of people who are your target audience and increase downloads for your app directly. You can also use this to re-engage with people who've already downloaded your app but don't use it much anymore.

Video Views

This is a new form of ad that Twitter is developing. It is in beta version as of writing of this book. It is similar to what Facebook has done where your native video will be automatically played in the tweet and the user will just have to un-mute it to listen to the sound. It is great for getting engaging content out in front of potential customers and followers.

Followers

This type of ad allows you to grow your number of followers directly. Your account will be promoted on the "who to follow" sidebar as well as on the timeline in the form of tweets that you can choose from existing tweets or create new ones especially designed to get people to follow you. Your account will also be shown on search results when someone searches for a keyword related to your business. You will pay on average $2-$3 per follower as per the current bidding rates. This is not much especially when you are trying to increase your followers in the beginning. If you also combine this with a good marketing campaign for a product, you can get good return on investment as you pay for getting followers and then market and sell your products to them through unpaid tweets.

Leads on Twitter

This type of ad can have a direct sign up button and you can use it to get leads for your product. You can get email newsletter subscribers, or get people to pre order something, or get people to sign up to get updates when you launch your product. It is a good form of marketing with high ROI.

Success Tips for Twitter

Create more content jabs and less right hooks. Twitter is the best platform for jabbing and interacting with real people in a real way. This will help you build real connections. Twitter can be used as a pretty good right hook platform as well but learn to keep it to the minimum. The 80/20 rule should be kept in mind here. Tweet non-advertorial content 80% of the time. Interact with people. Don't just tweet but reply and retweet and favorite.

Keep your brand voice in mind while tweeting. Don't be inconsistent with your tone. If you are mostly serious and then suddenly tweet something sarcastic or humorous, people might misunderstand.

Be interesting and human. It is possible to be boring even in 140 characters. Some people constantly tweet about what they are doing at that moment. Unless you are a celebrity, it's going to be boring for your followers to know your day to day routine. Unless you have something interesting or important to say, don't tweet. It is better to tweet less but tweet quality.

Find how you can provide value to your followers. Maybe you can tweet about interesting deals on your products. Or talk about a topic that is relevant to your followers. Share interesting articles and links. Share your own articles as well but don't keep pushing only your own blog posts all the time.

Use Twitter search to keep an eye on keywords related to your business. Whenever you find an opportunity, jump in with a comment. Twitter is a great place to find new people in this way. Suppose you sell washing machines and you find two people talking about your competitor's washing machines that are giving them trouble. You can jump in and suggest them to try your washing machines instead.

When using this strategy remember to not sound too intrusive. It is okay to jump into conversations this way on Twitter but still if you sound too obnoxious and push your products too much, you might not get a good response. Instead try to genuinely add your two cents to the conversation.

Use images with your tweets whenever possible to increase the area covered by your tweet. The twitter feed moves fairly quickly so if you have images you capture a large area on the page and your tweet becomes more visible.

Social Media Marketing

You can upload up to 4 images in the same tweet. This comes up as a collage of pictures which is much more interesting. Find creative ways to use this feature to market your content.

Learn Twitter terminology. Use RT while retweeting someone. MT stands for modified tweet and should be used while retweeting something that you've changed or shortened. If someone asks you to DM them, it means to send a direct message. Direct messages can only be sent between people who follow each other.

A lot of people use automated DM services. These services will send an automated direct message to anyone who follows you back. These messages often contain a thank you along with a link to whatever it is these people are selling. This is not a good thing to do as it will annoy most real people out there.

If you want to reply privately to someone use direct messages but **if you want to publicly reply to their tweet just hit reply** which will automatically add their Twitter handle in front of your tweet and link your reply to the original tweet. If you start a new tweet with @name that tweet will be visible to anyone who follows both you and the person mentioned in that tweet. If you want to mention someone but want that tweet to be visible to all your followers then don't start the tweet with @name. Instead put @name in the middle of the tweet or start the tweet with a period such as .@name.

Learn to use hashtags. Any word or phrase starting with a # sign becomes a hashtag. Find out the common hashtags such as #ff which stands for Friday Follow and is used to recommend interesting accounts on Fridays. Indie writers use #amwriting when talking about their books. Find the hashtags used in your industry.

Another way of using hashtags is to use trending hashtags to talk about topics that are relevant to your business. A lot of businesses will even use unrelated hashtags to promote their content. To do this successfully you need to keep an eye on the trending topics section of Twitter. Use your creativity to come up with ways to comment on interesting topics that are trending at the moment, even if they don't directly relate to your business. It will take a little creativity how you can comment on something unrelated to your business while still reminding people about your products. Of course, if you can't connect trending topics to your products, just tweet about what you think about each topic. Let it be a content jab. If it's funny and interesting, you might start an interaction with a few people that you would have never targeted through your ads.

When you start following a lot of people it can get hard to manage your feed. That's where Twitter lists come in handy. **Make lists to arrange the people you follow in appropriate categories.** You can also use lists to curate content from important people from your industry and offer these lists to your followers. For example if you are a fitness trainer, you can make a list of all the fitness gurus on Twitter and tell your followers to subscribe to your list to get the best fitness advice without having to follow hundreds of gurus.

Social Media Marketing

You can also use lists to mine for interesting people to follow. Subscribe to other people's lists and go through the members of that list to find more people to follow. If someone adds you to a list, go through the rest of the list to find more people like you in the same area of interest and interact with them to build your status as an influencer.

You can use several tools to enhance your Twitter experience. Apps like Buffer allow you to schedule your tweets so that you are tweeting at the right time. You can distribute tweets throughout the day instead of tweeting everything within a few minutes. You can also use apps like Followerwonk to understand your followers and how to best create engaging tweets for them.

Scheduling tweets is a slightly controversial topic. Here is the dilemma. Almost 500 million new tweets are tweeted every day on Twitter! Combine this with the real time nature of the feed and it means that the chance of people seeing your tweets is very less. They have to be online at the time that you are tweeting in order to see your tweet. Not all of your followers will be from the same time zone and so not all of them will see the tweet. To overcome this, a lot of people began the practice of scheduling the same tweet to tweeted several times during the day. So your chance of catching most of your followers increases.

But what about those people who don't follow a lot of people? Most real world users only follow a handful of people and their timelines are not that crowded. These people will see all of your tweets and they will be annoyed by your tweeting the same thing over and over again. This reduces the value you are providing to such followers and instead you become a nuisance.

And when everybody starts using this strategy, we come back to square one. The chance of your tweet being seen is again reduced and only the content on Twitter is bloated. The more bloating there is, the less your content will be seen. To solve this, Twitter has introduced the "while you were away..." section. So if you are a favorite account of your followers, they will be shown your tweets that they missed while they were offline. It is a good strategy to not go too deep into scheduling the same tweet 4-5 times a day. Instead tweet different and interesting things and build a strong relationship with your followers so when they miss something, twitter shows it to them when they come back.

Use Twitter cards for more visibility. As mentioned earlier, Twitter offers several types of cards. These cards need to be associated with a URL on your website, like the home page or the product page and whenever anyone tweets that URL as a link, their tweet will appear with your card. This will give that tweet more visibility and people can take action directly from the card.

Use Twitter analytics for understanding the reach of your tweets. Analytics is available to all Twitter accounts for free and you can see the engagement rate and the number of impressions for every tweet of yours. This will help you understand which tweets get most impressions and highest engagement so that you can improve your future content accordingly.

Social Media Marketing

Use Twitter Ads to promote your products. Apart from the ads mentioned above you can also use promoted trends. This will list your trend on top of the trending widget in the left sidebar and it is a good way to encourage users to engage with that hashtag and generate buzz for your product.

10 Common Social Media Mistakes on Twitter

Mistakes are commonplace; they are human nature and it's how we learn. Sadly, mistakes can be downright embarrassing and outrageous. One of the things you want in social media is for your business to be trending – but not for the wrong reasons. Social media marketing is all about customer engagement, listening to what they want and the ability to respond to them authentically. It is not about pushing your products, throwing too much information their way or ignoring their attempts to connect with you. As far as Twitter goes, there are best practices on how to generate engagement and clicks and there are bad practices. I am going to go over the 10 worst types of mistakes you can possibly make on Twitter.

Mistake #1: Tweeting "Buy This Product!"

Nobody likes to see their Twitter page full of tweets that are promoting this product or another. Yes, I know you are there to market your business but don't fall into the trap of tweeting things that are always all about you. Social media is, by its very definition, social. It is all about creating a dialogue between you and others so keep this in your mind when you are posting your tweets: more jabs and less right hooks.

Mistake #2: Begging People to Follow You

This is so not cool. Yes, all businesses want more followers because the more you have, the more your tweets get shared and the more they are reaching out to people. But don't be desperate about things; it really comes across quite badly. If you want more followers, earn them. Post content that is engaging, use your hashtags and show everyone that your business is one that everyone should want to be a customer of. If you want, you can use incentive schemes. Offer exclusive promotions to people who follow you on Twitter or run contests but, please, do not beg.

Mistake #3: Making Your Tweets Too Long

It might not sound much but using 140 characters for a Twitter post is too much. Although this is the maximum allowed, studies have shown that those posts that are kept below 100 characters tend to fare much better in the engagement stakes. Not only that, when a Tweet is too long, there is no room for you to add an @mention for easier sharing or for the post to be retweeted. Some of the tweets that have been shared the most are less than six words in total – Barack Obama's election tweet for 2012 springs to mind – "Four more years".

You do not need to use the entire 140 character limit for words, links and hashtags. Keep it short, keep it witty and keep it relevant.

Mistake #4: Not Responding to an @Mention

Social Media Marketing

Always keep an eye on your @connects when you have a business Twitter handle. Twitter is one of the best platforms to use for customer service and most of your customers probably do use it instead of using their email to contact you. Loads of businesses are found on twitter so if you are in a B2B, keeping in touch with people who contact you is simply courteous. If you can't be bothered or keep forgetting to check, your business is going to get itself a bad reputation with people thinking that you simply don't care about your customers.

Mistake #5: Tweeting the Same Thing All Day Long

Don't do it, really. You have no idea how monotonous and boring it is to find your Twitter notifications are saying the same thing all day long. It's spam for a start, annoying and completely unnecessary. It is also the fastest way to lose your followers and your business. This is a mistake generally made by new, smaller businesses who don't really know how to use Twitter properly. If you have one objective – to promote a specific campaign – then make your tweets interesting to read and vary them a little bit. Certainly do not tweet the same thing five times in a day. Mix things up, get people to interact with you and join in, instead of hitting the Unfollow button.

Mistake #6: Posting Too Many Random Retweets

Retweeting is a good practice to get yourself into. Use it to thank a customer or give another company much deserved praise but don't overdo it. Keep your retweet tactics in line with your marketing strategy. Make sure what you retweet reflects your brand and your habit on twitter. Certainly, do not use retweets as a replacement for your own content.

Mistake #7 Using Too Many Hashtags

This is a real common mistake among newbies. Too many hashtags can make it very difficult to read your post and it also says to people that you are not particularly focused on your message. As a general rule of thumb, stick to a maximum of three hashtags in one tweet. If you want to use more, use them in different updates.

Mistake #8: Tweeting too Quickly

People who over tweet about themselves, quickly lose followers and customers, especially those who seem to spend all day on twitter and hit the Post button every ten minutes. Stop. Think about what you are doing before you frighten everyone off with careless irrelevant tweets. Stick to a guideline of no more than eight tweets in a day unless you have something really special to tell your customers.

Mistake #9: Auto-Tweets

This practice is very similar to marmite – you either love it or you hate it. If you are using a management system for your social media marketing strategy and your tweets are pre-scheduled, make sure you are still monitoring your account.

Social Media Marketing

Auto tweeting can be the cause of some serious blunders, blunders that can have a detrimental effect on your business.

Mistake #10: Do Not Mix Up Your Twitter Handles!

This is for those of you that own multiple accounts. Be aware of which handle you are using to post what. Accidental posting of personal business using your business handle can hurt your business in a big way so keep your eyes open and your wits about you – and keep business and pleasure separate!

7 Steps to Using Hashtags Effectively

Most people already know what a hashtag is but for those who don't, they were first introduced on IRC's. These are Internet Relay Chats, a kind of live messaging and chat system that was the precursor to the social sites that we use today. Twitter made them popular where they were used as "tweet chats" which are like open group discussions on a specific topic. The very essence of tweet chats is still very relevant in the way that marketers use hashtags today.

A hashtag is a word or a series of words that come after the # sign. Those of you that are more technically inclined would probably call them metadata tags and they are a way of engaging your brand with your customers.

Knowing what hashtag you want to use is one thing; using it properly is another thing altogether. The following seven steps will show you how to use hashtags effectively in your social media marketing campaign:

1. Get the basics right

Hashtags that are complicated are not very friendly to the search engines. If you want to use a number in your hashtag you can make sure it is built in somehow - #2012 wouldn't do anything but #50ShadesofGrey does. If you are creating a hashtag that is specific to your brand, you can actually trademark it. But remember that creating your own hashtags is not the only way to go. You can also use popular generic hashtags to promote your products. Also, be aware that there are some characters, such as spaces and punctuation that are not allowed in a hashtag.

2. Test it before you finalize it

Test how effective your hashtag is by seeing what's already on the market. The last thing you want to happen after expending all that time and energy into coming up with the wittiest hashtag there is, is to find there is already something out there that uses it. If you can repurpose the existing hashtag to suit your own products, it can be an effective way of marketing. But it can also lead to backlash from the original community that was using that hashtag in a different way.

3. Get the timing right

*"The only reason for time is so that everything doesn't happen at once" –
Einstein.*

These words are plenty relevant here. As hashtags are generally used in tweets, it is important that you get the timing of your tweets right. Take the Australian branch of Random House Publishing. They were accused of all sorts of things after they sent a number of tweets, with the hashtag #LestWeForget, talking about a war-themed book. Nothing wrong with that, right? Except that they were sent during a one minute silence, effectively enraging customers.

4. It Takes Two to Hashtag

Twitter is another of those two-way streets we talked about. Hashtags help you to connect with people and to create a conversation point. Make sure that people can use your hashtag and turn it into a trending hashtag. The whole reason you want to create a hashtag is so that people can engage with your brand and talk about your brand with each other.

5. Make Sure You Use Your Hashtags Responsibly

There are rules to everything in life and trending topics are no different. As a rule, the message is to keep your hashtags relevant and appropriate. If you use irrelevant hashtags, you just draw attention to yourself and end up driving traffic away – fast.

6. Make Sure Your Hashtags Can be Customized for A Personal Experience

The big brands know how to make a hashtag personal to their users. Take the Bailey's Women's Prize for Fiction campaign on Twitter. They used a simple hashtag - #ThisBook - and asked people to share good fiction with everyone. Here is plenty of room for user-generated content and no room for going wrong.

7. Keep a Weathered Eye on Your Hashtag

Once your hashtag is out there in public, make sure you keep an eye on how users respond to it and how you can use it to respond to them.

Chapter 7
Google+

When Google+ began, people were reluctant to join and wanted to wait and see how it goes before they invested their time in it. At first it seemed to be just a mixture of Facebook and Twitter but there are enough unique value propositions offered by Google+ and today it is one of the top social networks. As of the last update provided by Google in October 2013, Google+ had 300 million monthly active users. The overall number of account holders on Google is well over 2 billion but these include accounts that are created automatically when someone opens a Gmail account or YouTube account.

In fact some people even feel that the 300 million active users figure is also bloated. A lot of these users are people who comment on YouTube and it gets shared automatically on their Google+ profile. So why join Google+ at all?

Why You Should Join Google+

Google+ integrates with all other Google products such as Search, Adwords, YouTube, Google Maps, Picassa, Gmail etc. If you combine the number of people using all these services it is clear that almost everyone who's online uses Google in one form or another. This means that your Google+ profile can potentially have unlimited reach.

If you can't get to people directly using Google+, posting on it and getting good engagement on it, can help you drive more traffic to your website by increasing your search engine ranking on Google search. Google search gives a lot more importance to a +1 on G+ than a like on Facebook. This is obvious because they want to promote people to use their own social network. In terms of SEO for your blog or website, G+ is a great network to be active on.

Google+ Hangouts are a great tool for marketers and you can't find anything similar on any other social network. You can have live Hangouts on Air and they'll stream live on your YouTube channel as well. While Webinar services charge you based on how many people watch your webinar, Hangouts can have unlimited viewers and all for free. Hangouts are great for marketers because you can connect with customers, both existing and prospective ones, almost face to face. There is nothing better than that in sales.

+Post Ads are a great feature for marketers, which allow you to turn your Google+ posts into ads that are shown by the Google Display Network just like other Adword ads. The difference is that if the viewer of the ad is on Google+, they can engage with the ad and +1 it or share it right from the ad.

Another reason to join G+ is that it is not as big as Facebook yet. So you actually have a lot more organic reach for your business on G+, even despite the smaller number of active users. If you remember Facebook posts by business pages can have an organic reach of as low as 2%. As G+ grows, those who already have a presence on it, will do much better than those who try to jump on the wagon after it has already passed them.

These few unique features of Google+ put up a compelling reason to give it a try. Here are some tips to make the most of it.

Understanding Google+

There are a lot of different features on G+. Let's go over them one by one.

Pages

Any business can create a G+ page. It is almost exactly similar to a Facebook page. Any business, product, brand, organization, artist etc. can create a G+ page. When you create your page, you can then use G+ just like a personal profile. You can post stuff, comment, +1, join or create communities etc. You can have a personal profile and a business page both.

The benefit of having a business page is that you can get deeper insights into your posts and use that page to promote your business and market your products.

Communities

Communities are similar to Facebook groups. It is a forum for people who have a shared interest. You can create a community for you customers or fans. You can join communities that are of interest to you. Any member of the community can post inside the community. You can have moderators to control the type of content that is posted along with having clear guidelines for posting content. Communities are a great way to develop a deep level of engagement with your customers.

Collections

G+ has introduced a new feature called collections. Basically you can create a collection around a certain topic and whenever you post about that topic you can add it to your collection. People can follow collections and every new post in that collection will be shown on their homepage. They can click on that post and jump to the collection to read other posts by that author on that topic in that collection.

This allows for a deeper level of engagement with fans and customers. People can now choose to follow just the topic that they are interested in. As a social media marketer you would do well to create relevant collections and then post in them regularly.

Circles

Circles are similar to Twitter lists. When you follow someone you can add them in a circle. You can create as many circles as you want. People can't see what circle you've added them in and they only get the notification that you've added them to their circles. So you can use circles to separate people into organized lists. You can share content with specific circles.

For example, you can create a circle for prospective clients and one for existing ones. So you can share some content with everyone and share the promotional posts only with the prospective clients. You can create highly targeted posts and share them with targeted circles.

You can even share your G+ posts with individual people directly. When you share with an individual's email id, they get an email about it. This can be a good way to make sure that your highly targeted post is seen by whoever you have targeted. But if you do this for all of your posts, you might be considered a spammer.

Events and Hangouts

You can organize real life events and use G+ to invite people. One good feature is that when the people who attend your event, go back and upload pictures of that event, they get shared at the same place for the entire event. In this way you can share perspectives of hundreds of people to your page. It will make the participants feel special and improve your image as a brand.

You can organize virtual events in the form of hangouts. You can invite people to participate in your hangout or just view it. Hangouts on Air lets you publish your live video content on the web for people to view for free. Anyone can join a live hangout on air. You can even upload the video of the hangout on YouTube so people can watch it later. People can comment on your live hangout and ask you questions which you can answer in real time. Hangouts are really powerful for marketers who know how to use them correctly. It depends on what type of content you are creating but with a little creativity you can find a way to utilize hangouts in your marketing strategy.

Success Tips for Google+

Like every other social network, you need to **provide value to your audience**. In Google+ it can be in the form of informative posts, links to your blog posts, interesting pictures, videos, community posts, polls, quizzes, hangouts etc. Remember the 80/20 rule about jabs and right hooks. More content that is not a direct sales pitch but instead is relevant to your audience and helps them with information or entertainment. G+ has a strong sense of community so when you become part of a community you need to uphold the standards of the community and share interesting and high quality content that is not too obvious as a sales pitch.

Create a business page or stick to your personal profile but **remember to use communities**. Either create communities around your product or join existing communities in your niche. You can find influencers on such communities and if you can impress them with your products, it can lead to a sharp rise in followers and customers.

Pages are especially great for small local businesses. You can create an entry on Google Maps and when someone in your locality is searching for the service you provide, they'll see your page on Google Maps. Your real life customers can like and review your establishment. You can also create a community around your patrons and offer special offers to community members.

Google+ is great for sharing pictures because unlike other social networks it doesn't autocrop the pictures to make them fit a standard box. You can use this feature to upload large pictures and they'll cover a large area on your page to grab the attention of the audience. G+ also allows for very large cover pictures that can make your page attractive and help in creating a good brand image.

There is no character limit on G+ so you can create longer posts. But remember that too long text based posts are not very exciting or attention grabbing. Use a good mix of an exciting image, an inviting headline and then more details in the text below. But don't turn it into a blog post. In fact a good way to share blog posts on G+ is to write a teaser in your post with a picture and the headline of the blog post and then add a read more link in the description.

Google allows you to format your posts by using certain variables. To bold text just close it in between "*". For italics use "_". And "-" for strikethrough. This allows you to direct users attention to the most important parts of the post. This is not possible on most other social networks. This also shows that Google has tried to guide users to use text based posts on their network. It certainly helps you with your SEO.

Social Media Marketing

You can tag people in your posts by using +name. Tagging allows for you to mention people in your posts so that you can encourage engagement and comments.

You can also use hashtags to increase the visibility of your posts. If you don't add tags, Google will automatically try to add the proper tags based on the content of your posts. But don't use too many hashtags on G+.

If you are active on YouTube, you have to be active on Google+ because of the wonderful integration between the two platforms. People can watch your YouTube videos directly on Google+. If they comment on Google+ it will also be added to the YouTube comments and if someone comments on YouTube it will show up as a shared post on their Google+ profile. You can live stream your hangouts on YouTube and they'll automatically be saved on YouTube for later viewing. So while you do live hangouts you are also creating content for your YouTube channel.

You can also embed posts on your website or blog. This allows users to interact with your Google+ profile right from your website. They can +1 the post, comment on it using their G+ profile, and even share it with their followers, right on your website or blog. If you don't want to embed posts you can embed a Google+ badge on your website that links to your page. This allows you to gather followers on G+ who just happened to be visiting your website. Usually you might not have managed to convert every visitor because not everyone signs up for your newsletter. But by having a G+ batch all they have to do is click on the follow button and they can easily add you to their circles. You can then add them back and you have literally generated a lead that can one day convert to a paying customer.

Use circles to sort people into relevant categories. By using this feature you can have both personal and business contacts in Google+. When you want to post something that only your friends and family see, you can post it just to that particular circle. As mentioned above, circles are a bit like Twitter lists but much more powerful than that. So use them creatively. Create targeted circles based on your particular needs. Maybe you can add male customers to one circle and females to another so that you can create targeted content for your male and female customers.

Use Ripples to measure and analyze your social outreach. It is a great inbuilt tool for analytics that is much easier and intuitive to read and understand than graphs and other statistics. Analytics let you hone your marketing strategy as you can tell which post did well and which one didn't do so well.

Use the power of hangouts to connect face to face with your customers. If you are wondering what kind of hangouts you can do, it's always good to do some educational hangouts where you share your expertise with the viewers. You can also interview interesting people from your industry. You can add up to 9 people to your hangout and interview them. Hangout is one of the most powerful tools offered by Google+ and it's completely free so make the most of it.

9 Social Media Mistakes on Google+

Google+ may well be one of the newest social media sites but it is an extremely powerful one. In fact, since its launch two years ago, it has overtaken Twitter and landed in behind Facebook as the second largest social media site in existence. So, why are so many people mired in confusion about how best to use it? Well, one of the reason as we mentioned above is that the numbers of G+ could be much more bloated than other networks because of the fact that other Google services are connected to it. Of course integration is also one reason why G+ can be very powerful.

Another reason why people aren't too keen on joining G+ is because of Google's reputation of killing projects out of the blue. They did that with Google Glass and Google Buzz (Does anyone remember Google Buzz?) and technically they could do it with G+ as well. But there are reasons to believe that they won't do it with G+.

One reason is that they are calling it a social layer underneath all of their other services instead of a stand alone social network. This means that they want it to be the core of their business. Also Google has restructured itself under an umbrella corporation called Alphabet. They did this because they wanted to separate the core Google products from the more radical research and development ones.

This will allow them to be more transparent about Google revenues to shareholders and the shareholders won't feel like they are investing in a company that is launches too many risky products. By separating the risky parts from the core parts, they've shown that they don't want to kill anymore of their projects.

But these reasons are still confusing to most people and so they either don't join G+ or they join it and never use it. Because of this, mistakes are being made and here we look at the top 9:

Mistake #1: Not Completing Your Profile Properly

If you are using Google+ as a business marketing tool, make sure you set up a business page – it will have a significant effect on your SEO rankings! It is simple to set up a Google+ page, similar in many respects to a business page on Facebook. You must have a personal Gmail address and account to open a business page and you must give your location, as well as giving your business a category.

If you do want to post from your personal account, you can but do make sure that your company is listed somewhere on it. Otherwise, you will not be able to link back or reference it in any way, not to mention all the other business things that raise your profile. When you are completing your profile, make sure you:

- Include business specific keywords in your introduction and your tagline – pick the ones you already use for your ranking now

- Use the golden opportunity that Google gives you to list all of your other social media sites

- Add your website address to your profile

All of this goes towards giving you better SEO and making it far easier for you to be found as well as being far more marketable to potential customers. Also, make sure you use the space provided to describe your business, your products or your services. Tell people whether they need to visit you in person or if they can buy online.

This is your chance to sell yourself – don't miss anything out!

Mistake #2: Stuffing Your Profile Full of Keywords

Yes, you need a certain amount of keywords in evidence but don't overdo it. Keyword stuffing does not increase your SEO ranking; rather it will have the opposite effect. Google doesn't like anything that looks like it may be spam and that's what keyword stuffing looks like.

When you complete your profile, write naturally, as if you were talking to people. Pay close attention to the details that you put in; include some product names or services that you offer. Not only will your customers love it, Google will too. And if Google loves you, you are on the track towards marketing success.

Mistake #3: Using a Poor Quality Cover Image

Google+ has recently had a bit of a design makeover and one of the changes they made was to allow users a bigger cover picture. Now you have to load an image that is no less than 480 pixels wide and 270 pixels high. The maximum size, which is the best size to use is 2120 x 1192 pixels – this will ensure that your image is clear. Also take into account the location you take your profile cover image in.

Don't use an image that is out of focus, grainy, not proportioned properly, or badly placed. There are many creative ways of using a cover image that creates brand identity and also sells your brand to prospective customers. Change cover image often to stay fresh but make sure that every image is true to your brand identity.

Mistake #4: Not Using Circles Properly

In Google+ terms, Circles are groups of connections and Google allows you to place your followers into segments so that you can better target your posts. You can generate new Circles for customers who shop in-store, online only customers, industry leaders, partners, coworkers, business friends, and so on.

Use them and use them well by targeting specific news to specific circles. If all of your followers are in just one circle then you are not using circles properly

Mistake #5: Flooding Your Circles with Spam

We know now what Circles are and how to use them but you must now learn not to abuse them. Let me give you an example; you may have a circle that is quite small, perhaps one for business associations. By all means, post an update via email to that Circle but do not then send them an email to tell them that you have sent them an update.

In a similar manner to Facebook, Google also uses algorithms to determine what posts will be seen by whom. Using the email option allows you to send important update to that specific circle, or to certain people with the circle. It's a great feature, just don't spam your circles, they won't thank you for it and nether will Google!

Mistake #6: Only Posting About You and Your Product

This is one of the biggest social media mistakes, no matter which site you are using. Social media is about interaction, it is about creating a dialogue between you and your customers. It is about networking, not banging on about yourself all day. People don't want to hang out with those who talk only about themselves and they don't want to receive constant updates that are only about your products or service.

There is an 80/20 rule in social media marketing – 80% of your business comes from 20% of the people and the same rule goes for posting. 80% of your posts should be content jabs: about general stuff, while 20% should be right hooks: about you and your company. It's called engagement and it is the number one reason for running a social media campaign in the first place.

Mistake #7: Ignoring the Negative Comments

This is another big no-no. If people make negative comments on your posts, you must respond to them. Bad comments happen; it's part and parcel of social media. At the end of the day, it's an open forum and not everyone has the same feelings or thoughts as you do; some people may not even like what you do.

When you are running a business, you take the rough with the smooth and you must keep on monitoring every single social media site you use. Be careful how you respond to comments, especially negative ones and make sure you listen to what is actually being said. Customers want to know that you are listening and, just occasionally, a person will post a bad comment just to test that. You must address negative concerns as quickly as you would positive ones and halt the tie of any negative feeling that may rise against your business. For example:

- If you get a comment made about a product, ask the commenter to email you with specific details so you can look into it.

- If you get a negative comment about you or your business, address it in such a way that you can try to turn it into a positive comment.

- If you get a negative comment about a specific post, at least try to talk to the commenter about it. You may not be successful but at least you will have tried.

- If the comment is inappropriate, delete it, but do warn the commenter that this is what you are doing first; otherwise, you may just end up with more bad publicity.

You can also report abusive or spam comments. This will help Google mark any profiles that are particularly for spamming or for trolling.

Mistake #8: Not Joining Up With Communities

Communities are one of the key features about Google+ so find the ones that suit your niche and join them. Communities are a relatively new thing, being introduced in 2012. They were a Google response to Facebook groups and to the hashtag communities on Twitter. They are however, growing rather quickly and can be incredibly engaging. Basically, a Google+ community is a way of finding other people in your niche and interacting with them.

You can search out relevant communities yourself or Google will send you recommendations based on your profile and on the updates that you post. If you can't find a community that suits, simply make one of your own and invite people to join you.

To be honest, if you are not using communities in some way or another, you are missing out on what could be a fantastic opportunity. Like everything else though, use them but don't abuse them. Don't spam them and don't talk only about yourself. Engage with others, get involved in their discussions and treat people like they are human beings and valued potential customers – they may well be a customer of yours one day so make the right impression form the outset.

Mistake #9: Posting Without Making any Comments

This may be last on the list but that doesn't make it any less important. Never ever, post a link without some kind of comment attached to it. It makes you look as though you haven't given any thought and this kind of post does not intend to engage people as they have absolutely no motivation to read it.

Chapter 8
LinkedIn

LinkedIn is the largest professional networking website in the world. It crossed 300 million users in April 2014. It is different from the rest of the social networks because it is a professional network. Some people only use LinkedIn as an online resume but it is much more than that.

LinkedIn is indispensible if you need to do B2B or business to business marketing. But other businesses and brands can also create a good reputation for their brand by using LinkedIn. Any business or brand needs to network with other businesses and professionals in the industry as well. LinkedIn is a great place to increase your reputation as an industry leader or influencer. If you offer B2B services, then LinkedIn is the best place for you to market your service. If you are a freelancer, you too can use LinkedIn to find new clients and increase your authority in your industry as a thought leader. If you need to hire people for you business, LinkedIn is a great place to find the right talent.

LinkedIn is moving fast to turn it into a more active social network instead of just a place people go to update their resume or look for jobs. You can now create posts and share them with your connections. This native content on LinkedIn is different from all other social networks. This content needs to be more professional and serious. Although, if your brand voice demands it, you can be funny as well. These posts are like articles in a newspaper and less like blog posts. If you can learn to master this native post on LinkedIn and use it creatively you can soon spread your influence in your industry.

There are also a lot of groups based around certain topics or interests. Join these groups and participate in them regularly. LinkedIn creates a rating for you as a group member. The more you participate in the group, that is creating posts, commenting, answering questions etc. the higher your rating goes. You can become an influencer in a group and that makes you an influencer that is visible to more people and more people would want to connect with you.

Success Tips for LinkedIn

Complete your profile thoroughly and honestly. If you are a business, set up a company page and fill all the information you can provide about your company. If you are an individual, fill it with your resume and your past work experience along with your current business information.

The tone you use to post content on LinkedIn has to be slightly more professional than other networks. If your brand voice is informal, maybe you can pull off being funny on LinkedIn but still you have to approach the content strategy with a little seriousness.

You don't need to share every post from your blog and all other social networks on LinkedIn. Only share those posts that are relevant to your professional network. Instead focus on creating native posts for LinkedIn but this too you don't have to do too often. The posting frequency for LinkedIn is longer than most other social networks. You can even do well with one well thought out post per month. Or even one in every few months. The quality is much more important than the quantity here.

Make use of the LinkedIn Publisher platform to write posts just for LinkedIn. But remember that the tone and matter of these posts have to be professional. Use this platform to build up your authority as a leader in your industry.

Use the LinkedIn cover image to increase visibility. You can have something eye catching or something that tells people more about your company.

Join Groups and participate in discussions related to your industry. Don't be self-promotional in-group discussions. You can ask other professionals in the group to review your product or take a look at your blog posts but remember that this is not a place to sell your products unless you have a B2B product. Even then, restrict direct selling on LinkedIn. It would be best to convert the 80/20 rule to more like 95/5 rule for LinkedIn.

You can also participate in LinkedIn Answers to answer questions posted by others and build up your reputation as an authority.

Build up your network by searching for influencers in your industry and connecting with them. But don't spam everyone you can find with a generic request. Take some time to learn about each person and send a personal message introducing yourself and the reason why you'd like to connect with them.

Use LinkedIn Advertising if you have a B2B business that you'd like to advertise on LinkedIn.

Hire the best talent from LinkedIn for your business. This is what the network was meant to do from the beginning. Check out references on LinkedIn when someone applies to your company for a job. Put out job posts directly on LinkedIn.

7 Social Media Mistakes on LinkedIn

LinkedIn has more than 300 million users and it provides some very valuable opportunities for networking for professionals. It is a social network but it is more geared towards business users, which means that people don't have to face the constant personal and public struggle that other social network sites tend to create.

When you join LinkedIn, you can join in with niches that are specific to your industry without having to get involved in a newsfeed that is filled with photographs of what your followers had for dinner that night.

It is a fantastic networking tool and it is the perfect platform for social media marketing. However, although LinkedIn pretty much maintains a professional environment, users can still make some rather large social blunders. The following are seven of the top mistakes that people make on LinkedIn:

Mistake #1: Not Actually Being on LinkedIn

When you are in business, possibly the single biggest mistake you can make is to avoid being on LinkedIn in the first place. A recent survey that was carried out asked just over 1000 people how they find information about potential services; almost 60% said that they used social media as their first port of call. The number one social media site that they use to check out potential business is LinkedIn, by a very large majority.

If you are one of the very last people making a stand and holding out on joining social media, it really is time to give in. LinkedIn is not a passing fad, it is not going to disappear without a trace and not using it could be one of the biggest mistakes you ever make in your business life.

Mistake #2: Not Completing Your Profile Fully

When you network face to face with prospective clients, you want to create a good impression. The same goes for LinkedIn. Your profile is the online version of your face to face meeting and it is very important that it is completed fully, with as much information as you can put in there. It isn't just your resume; it is where you are going to showcase your business, what you are good at, your specialties and your credentials. It is where you are going to talk about successful projects from the past and talk about things you are passionate about; this is where your personality comes to the fore and it is one of the first things that people look at on LinkedIn. Not completing it fully or properly can lead to a loss of potential business.

Mistake #3: Not Joining Relevant Groups

LinkedIn has lots of different groups and they are a fantastic way for professionals to network. Joining groups that are highly relevant to your niche or industry is a smart business move and it can provide you with loads of new connections and give your business a boost.

But joining groups will solve nothing unless you actively spend time on those groups. These are forums where you have to put in time and energy to participate. You need to introduce yourself when you join a group. Then you need to comment on other people's posts. Since it is like a forum it's not one time comment but rather a continuous conversation; and sometimes in real time. And finally you have to share your own insightful posts relevant to that group.

Mistake #4: Only Posting about Yourself

This is a common theme and it is the same principle with all social media sites. When you join groups on LinkedIn, it is important that your posts are not all about you. Other people in the group will soon lose interest once they realize you have no interest in them or what they are doing and are only happy to talk about yourself and your business. Follow the special 95/5 rule we created specifically for LinkedIn – 95% of your posts should be about relevant topics or discussions and 5% should be about you.

Mistake #5: Coming Across As Too Sales-Oriented

Ok, so the whole idea is to make sales but there is a way of doing it. If you constantly come across as self-promotional, you will very quickly turn people off your business. In some cases, it can actually result in you being banned from certain groups and that never looks good. The last thing you want is for people to write you off before you have been able to prove yourself and your product or service.

The very best way to avoid making this common mistake is to focus on relationship building first. Earn their trust, before you start talking about what you can do for each other.

Mistake #6: Not Using LinkedIn as a Business Development Tool

Because that is exactly what it is intended to be used for. You can use LinkedIn to send traffic to your website simply by sharing content that is relevant and by establishing yourself as a valuable resource on your profile. When people who have connected with you begin to see you as an expert who can be trusted, they will be more likely to give your business that same level of confidence.

Mistake #7: Not Creating a Really Great Company Page

As well as establishing yourself on LinkedIn with a great profile, you should also make sure that your company has its own page as well. You can use Showcase pages where it is appropriates as a way of keeping all your information organized.

Never be afraid of telling people that your company has a page on LinkedIn and try to encourage them to follow you so that they can be kept fully up to date on what you are doing. We already know that prospective customers look for an online presence so it is important that your company have a really strong profile on LinkedIn.

Never allow mistakes such as these to throw your social media marketing campaign off course. If you have already committed a few of these, don't worry about it, just put it right now.

Social Media Marketing

There are of course hundreds of other social networks as well but you should remember that you need to be where your audience is. So if your audience is on a small niche social network then by all means go there.

Remember the golden rule of providing real value to your followers and you'd do well on any social network. But the corollary of providing real value is that you can't be active on too many social networks and still provide value on all of them. Of course, if you have a big business with a team of social media managers, then you can manage multiple networks.

Chapter 9
YouTube

Videos are the most engaging form of content on the internet. Articles ask for a lot of concentration from the readers. Pictures are more absorbing but to communicate something you have to return to written words. Videos are the most addictive form of content. We all know how time can fly while watching a movie.

As a social media marketer you can drive a lot of engagement through videos. You can drive traffic to your website or advertise and even sell products directly through videos. The only problem with this great form of content is that it is not that easy to produce valuable videos.

Valuable Videos

What I mean by valuable videos is the type of videos that provide some form of value to the viewers. This is not about producing high quality, professionally edited, Hollywood style videos. With the technology and information that we have today, it is very easy to produce decent quality videos. But the value part comes in when you think about the content of those videos.

Mostly, valuable videos provide either information about something or entertainment in some form. Great videos do both.

Before you think about getting into videos as a marketing tool, you have to assess whether your content is suited to the video format and whether or not you can consistently produce valuable videos.

YouTube Vs Vimeo

If you do decide to get into videos there are two big sites to choose from: YouTube and Vimeo. YouTube is the number one choice for most video producers. In terms of numbers, YouTube far outshines Vimeo. YouTube has over 1 billion users. Videos on YouTube get 4 billion views per day and about 100 hours of videos is uploaded to YouTube every minute! In comparison Vimeo only has about 175 million viewers.

The main difference between YouTube and Vimeo is that Vimeo was started by a bunch of filmmakers and even today it deals with more artistic and better produced videos. The Vimeo site is designed to enhance the video watching experience of the viewers with a large video player that is great for HD videos.

There are no ads before or during the videos, like on YouTube. The viewers on Vimeo are also more interested in the art of filmmaking than on YouTube.

If you are a filmmaker then Vimeo makes complete sense for you. But if you are a social media marketer trying to get traffic to your website or sell products, then YouTube is your best choice. Since for most people YouTube is the network of choice, I'll only talk about tips related to YouTube.

The Power of YouTube

YouTube is a unique content creation site. The videos on YouTube range from a random video blog shot through a low resolution webcam to heavily produced movies and entertainment shows. YouTube is different from all other social networks because when the other networks came along, people found a new dimension to life. These networks created a new niche for themselves in people's lives. But YouTube is the only one which took over the niche that was ruled by television until then.

Today people visit YouTube to be entertained and educated. Individuals with minimum budgets are taking on big budget media houses to fight for the limited attention span of the audience. And the individuals are winning. YouTube has not just taken over TV but it has redefined entertainment itself. Boring soap operas that never ended are out. Even 45 minute episodes of drama broken up by 15 minutes of forced advertisements are out. What's in are short videos loaded with entertainment, without even a few seconds of fluff.

The audience now expects videos to capture their attention from the get go and never let it go. If they slacken up for even a few seconds, the audience will stop watching and click on one of the many similar videos listed on the side. This is why YouTube is a challenging but powerful content creation site.

YouTube is also a search engine. The content creators are in millions but there are even more people who use the site just for content search and consumption. When you search something on Google, they show one or two relevant videos related to those keywords. You can also choose to only search for videos. When you do that, you'll find that almost all the videos are on YouTube. Not just that, most people open YouTube and then search within it for "how to" videos and music videos and movie trailers and so on and so on. This is why being on YouTube is important if you can create valuable videos related to your niche.

Finally, YouTube is also a social network. The comment sections of YouTube are used more than any other social network. You can get a lot of organic engagement on YouTube. Because of this reason YouTube comments are also the most honest reflection of the internet. You'll find as many hateful and negative comments as good ones. But if you take the time to manage your comments, you can use it to create incredible value for your customers. You can build a strong fan base that eagerly waits for your new videos.

These three factors make this site unique and powerful. Sure you can search on Facebook and Twitter as well but most people don't use these sites for searching. You can create videos on Facebook and through Vine on Twitter as well, but if your marketing strategy is based around serious video content then you have to be on YouTube. You create your videos on YouTube and then share them on other social networks. You can even embed the videos on your blog or website.

Basic Concepts of YouTube

Anyone can sign up on YouTube. Even if you are not a content creator you can sign up. When you sign up, you automatically create a channel. Channels are where you can post your videos. One account can have multiple channels. A lot of users create different channels for different topics that they want to talk about.

You can create playlists from your own videos and from other YouTube videos. When you like a video, it is added to an automatically generated playlist for all of your favorite videos. Playlists can help you arrange subtopics in your channel so that viewers can find them easily.

You can edit your videos by using the inbuilt editor. You can add sounds and music to your videos using the free audio library provided by YouTube. You can add closed captions for viewers of different languages. You can add annotations which make the video interactive. For example, you can add a box that links to your website or to your product's landing page. In the video you can encourage people to click on the box. In this way you can create call to action buttons on your video and trust me, a video call to action is quite literally a "call" to action and works much better than words typed over a button.

You can also create cards that direct the viewers to some other video or even an outside link such as your website. There are powerful ways to use the YouTube video editor and you can learn more about it through different videos available on the site.

You can monetize your channel. This is a feature that once again makes YouTube unique. You can become a partner with YouTube and earn money through advertisements shown on your videos. If you have a large following, you can earn a good amount of money through YouTube. It's not just a way to market your products but even to make some money!

The analytics provided by YouTube are also extremely powerful. You can get a lot of information about your viewers from YouTube. Use this knowledge to see what demographic is watching your videos and find out if it is your target demographic or not.

Success Tips for YouTube

Create valuable content. It doesn't have to be of very high production quality but it needs to provide value to your audience, either in the form of entertainment or information. Of course it doesn't mean that it's okay to put out very low quality videos. At least make sure that the audio quality is good. People will tolerate grainy video but they won't tolerate bad sound.

Create content regularly. The top channels on YouTube publish videos regularly. Some channels publish several videos everyday while others publish once a month. It all depends on the type of videos you are making. Most of the time the more frequently you publish the better it will be. But you should have a realistic publishing schedule; something you can stick to easily. One video per week, on a fixed day every week, is a good frequency to have. It creates expectation from your viewers about new content every week.

Use your creativity to come up with something unique. Remember that 100 hours of video is uploaded every minute on YouTube. What sets your content apart from others? Have a unique selling proposition. Even if you are targeting a very particular niche, try to create something original. How you do this will depend entirely on what products you are trying to market and how creative you are.

Reply to comments and engage with your audience. YouTube has a bad reputation when it comes to comments as there can be a lot of spam or abusive comments and many popular channels disable comments because it can get very hard to manage them properly. There is nothing wrong with disabling comments but if you have them enabled then moderate them regularly and reply back to genuine people. It is great to see engagement in comments below your videos. When someone is trolling, you'll see that other viewers will step in to defend you. In a way the comment section creates brand loyalty in the genuine viewers.

Use your brand image for your channel art and link it to your other social network profiles. The cover image on YouTube shows up very differently on mobile and on TV. Remember that a lot of people now watch YouTube videos on their television sets which can connect to the internet. Take some time to create a cover image that looks good on all three formats. When you create the cover YouTube will show you all three previews. The way to achieve this is to have the most important content of the cover in the center.

It's not enough to produce valuable videos but you also have to **market these videos on your other social networks**. Use your social networks to drive traffic to your videos and your videos will drive traffic to your website. If your videos are more than just marketing videos, but part of your money generating content, then you have to market them on other social networks even more so.

Social Media Marketing

If you are a freelancer or an indie artist, share your knowledge and experience in your videos. Artists of course also share their art. There is a large community of indie musicians on YouTube for inspiration.

If you get enough traffic you can also join YouTube's partner program and earn decent revenue from advertisements on your videos.

Data has shown that viewers decide in the first 15 seconds whether they are going to invest their time in the video or not. So put compelling and enticing content in the first 15 seconds. A lot of people now put a hook in the opening 15 seconds that engages the audience. The intro is pushed back to after the hook.

Start your videos with a custom animated intro. It gives the impression of a professional YouTube channel and people will stay with your video for longer. You can even have a 15 second preview of the most interesting parts of the video and then go to the intro so that viewers know what is coming in the video even before the intro. There are plenty of websites such as <u>VideoHive</u> or <u>SmartShoot</u> that allow you to create a professional animated introduction.

End your videos with call to actions. You can simply ask your viewers to like, share and subscribe the video. You can also use annotations to create clickable banners on the video that will direct your viewers to your website or to a landing page for your product. Asking people to like, share and subscribe can have a big difference in engagement. Sometimes people might like your videos but just avoid subscribing because of laziness. When you ask someone to do something, they are more likely to oblige.

Keep SEO in mind and use proper keywords in your video title, description and tags. Also remember that the first few lines of the description are the most important because that's what's normally visible on YouTube. To read the complete description the viewer has to click on "read more" so give them a reason to do so in the first few lines.

Give proper attribution for any copyrighted content that you might have used in your videos, in the description. YouTube is big on enforcing copyrights and if your videos contain scenes from movies or other shows, then make sure to attribute it in the description.

Be ready to spend years on YouTube. Consistent high quality content over many years will make your channel popular. The returns you get will grow exponentially. Only one of your videos has to go viral and when that happens all of your previous videos will get a lot of views as well. So keep creating high quality content and do it in a way that you enjoy it. If you enjoy it, you can do it for a long time even if your growth is not satisfactory. Keep at it, and one day it will be.

5 Social Media Mistakes on YouTube

The path to success is never a smooth one and the one that leads to YouTube success is filled with potholes of all shapes and sizes. A small business that is just starting out, who perhaps only has a small budget, cannot afford to fall into any of these holes and the only way to stay out of them is not to make some of the more basic errors. YouTube is a very powerful tool in social media marketing and can gain you many hundreds or thousands of new leads. The following five mistakes are those that you definitely should not make:

Mistake #1: Having Unrealistic Expectations

You hear so much about YouTube, about how people have made a small fortune on there and some businesses believe that they only have to upload one video to gain millions of viewers. It doesn't work like that and it is a very rare video that catches enough attention to send it viral.

Bear in mind that, every single minute, more than 100 hours of video content is being uploaded to YouTube, making the competition extremely stiff. You must have realistic expectations of what YouTube can do for your business and how long it will take. And it isn't just about uploading that video and then sitting back, waiting for success to fall into your lap. You must promote that video, and promote it hard. Get yourself set up on other social media sites first and get your feet settled there before you head to YouTube. At least then, you will have a solid audience to promote your video to.

Mistake #2: Thinking Too Small

This maybe goes against what we just said above but, although you must keep your expectations realistic, don't think that, just because you are only a small business, that success on YouTube can't be yours. There are lots of small brands who believe that they have to be one of the bigger brands to get anywhere and that simply isn't true. When it comes to YouTube, it isn't about who has the well-known brand, it's about quality and it's about making a video that people want to see.

Mistake #3: Treating Your YouTube Video as a Commercial

YouTube is relatively new as a social media channel and it personifies engagement. When you upload a video, you should do it with the thought in mind that you are doing more than just selling your product or service. If you can do that, you are ahead of the game already. YouTube is about having fun so don't slam a load of promotional sales pitch videos on the table. It certainly isn't a dumping ground, every video that you post must represent your brand in personality, and it must provoke some kind of reaction from your audience.

As far as jabs and right hooks goes, YouTube is best for combining the two. You can create powerful jabs that have a right hook right at the end. Your jabs can become your right hooks when your videos start getting so many views that you can earn some money through them. As long as the video is high quality and provides real entertainment or education, people won't mind if you place a sales pitch right at the end.

But don't make it too needy. Just ask people to click on your link to know more about your products. That's about as much sales as you can do. Once in a while you can also create out and out sales videos, for example, to introduce a new product. But don't expect such videos to go viral or generate subscribers to your channel.

Mistake #4: Limiting Yourself to YouTube

While YouTube is the largest video media channel on the internet, it most certainly isn't the only one and it may not be the best choice for your particular brand. Think about signing up to others – Vimeo is the idea choice for creative people, for example. If you are looking to spread the word about your business, explore the world that exists beyond the standard social media channels and utilize a number of different methods.

Mistake #5: Counting Views As your Only Success marker

So often, people upload a video to YouTube and keep their fingers crossed that this one will be the one to get 1 million views. These days, success isn't counted in views, it's the reaction that your video gets that is important. If you don't engage your audience, you can get 5 million views and it still won't make you a superstar.

Look at how many times your video has been shared on other social media sites as well; this is usually a pretty good measure of how successful it is.

Chapter 10
Instagram

Now let's talk about visual content in the form of pictures and infographics. There are two social networks that have gained popularity in a short amount of time by focusing on visual content. Pinterest and Instagram have millions of users interacting by sharing pictures. Marketers and businesses have found great success through these sites because visual content is much more engaging and captivates the audience.

Any type of business or creative individual can benefit from marketing on these sites because everyone takes pictures and sharing your pictures is a great way to bond with other people. While building your social media strategy you should seriously consider having either Instagram or Pinterest as one of your social networks. You can even have both the sites as they are quite different from one another. We'll talk about Pinterest in the next chapter. Right now let's focus on Instagram.

Basics of Instagram

Instagram began as an app for iOS but has now grown into a social network with over 300 million monthly active users. People share their pictures along with a description of the picture. Their followers can like and comment on the picture. Everyone from top brands to individual marketers use Instagram in unique and creative ways to market their products.

Instagram is special in the way that people can only create content through their phones. Which means that most people view Instagram on their phone. So when you are considering creating content for this site, make sure to keep the mobile screen size in mind.

Instagram provides picture editing tools along with some great filters. It allows people without much knowledge or experience in photography to post stunning shots on their Instagram page. This is a major factor in the success of this site. Make sure your pictures are artsy and creative. These are the kinds of pictures that do well.

Selfies and group pictures, behind the scenes pictures also do well. Pictures with text and infographics don't do well on Instagram. As you'll read in the next chapter, they do quite well on Pinterest and that's why you can use both networks in your marketing strategy.

Social Media Marketing

Hashtags work better on Instagram than any other site, including Twitter. On this site it is okay to load your description with as many relevant hashtags as you want. It will increase exposure and help you gain new followers.

After Facebook bough Instagram, it was speculated that the site will be "Facebookised" with lots of ads and irrelevant content. But Instagram has stayed true to its core and has gone back to a minimal theme. Instagram also launched a video service which allows people to share videos just like they were sharing pictures. Creative social media marketers are finding unique ways to use videos on Instagram to market their products.

Instagram is a great place for creating content jabs and building a following. It is great for engaging with people. It is good for bringing people back to your website. It is not so good for right hook content that out and out sells a product. So keep this in mind while considering Instagram from your social media marketing strategy.

Success Tips for Instagram

You can share different types of content on Instagram. If you are an independent creative like a musician or an author you can even share your day to day pictures so that your fans can feel connected to the real you. You can share creative pictures that represent your point of view. You can write a few words that describe what the picture is about. You can also share mood pictures to share how you are feeling at that moment.

If you are a business you can **share behind the scenes pictures** with your customers to let them get to know how your business runs. For a brand it can be hard to use Instagram because it is so much better suited for individuals. One way to use it is to let workers share their pictures on your Instagram feed.

You should **share professional and stunning pictures** that will provide esthetic value to your audience. If you know nothing about photography, spend some time learning the basics of composition and light. Frame your pictures in a good way using the rule of thirds. And use Instagram filters to give them that professionally edited look.

Businesses can **share pictures of their products**. For example, you can have a daily discount deal on a different product and share its picture so your followers can know which product to buy. But unless you do it extremely creatively, people might not like that you are always selling to them. So do it as infrequently as possible.

Infographics and pictures with a lot of written content weren't much popular on Instagram but are starting to be accepted. People are using pictures to post quotes, memes and even simple steps to do something, like an exercise routine or a recipe. Still, if this type of content is your main forte than Pinterest would be much better suited to your needs.

You can create competitions on Instagram to engage with the audience. You can have a competition where people need to like a picture to enter a lucky draw. You can also have a contest where users generate content and tag it with your hashtag to enter their pictures into the contest. This is a great way to engage with the audience and at the same time get tons of great user generated content to share on your page. You can even use contests to build email lists. All you need to do is ask for the email in the submission form for the contest.

Share videos on Instagram in creative ways. Maybe you can share behind the scenes footage or answer frequently asked questions. There is no limit to your creativity.

While choosing pictures for Instagram remember that it uses a square panel to show the pictures. So square pictures will cover the entire area, while landscape, rectangular pictures will be shown with borders on top and bottom.

Creating great content is not enough. You must also **engage with your audience**. Instagram comments section is great for chatting with your followers. Instagram Direct also allows you to take the chat private with up to 15 people. You can use this to address complains or have a secret insider chat!

Hashtags are used a lot on Instagram and can take your content to new viewers. So use hashtags intelligently with your posts. They should be relevant to your pictures. You can create your own hashtags for your brand or an ongoing competition or choose from the popular hashtags in your industry. Using hashtags for popular current events can also be a good way to reach new viewers. Use as many hashtags as you can as long as they are relevant to the content.

Find popular Instagrammers in your niche and engage with them. Follow them and build a genuine relationship with them. Get them to talk about you or your business. You can send free samples for review or even pay them cash to post your pictures on their feed and link back to your Instagram account. To find such Instagrammers search popular hashtags of your niche and find profiles that have a lot of followers. Usually you can tell if someone posts sponsored pictures by looking through their feed. Or you can contact them and simply ask.

Use your other social networks to drive traffic to Instagram. Share Instagram pictures on Facebook and Twitter. Twitter doesn't show Instagram pictures in the timeline. It only shows a link. But by using IFTTT (IF This Then That) service you can use a recipe that automatically shares all Instagram pictures as native pictures on Twitter. We'll talk more about IFTTT in Part 3 of this book.

8 Social Media Mistakes on Instagram

Instagram came into existence in 2010 and since then it has grown quickly. It gives businesses the opportunity to tell their story through visual aids. Instagram was bought by Facebook which is now the proud owner of 300 million accounts. Every single day, around 150 million people use Instagram and they spend, on average, about 21 minutes using the app. The top brands have grasped this fact and very quickly realized that Instagram has huge potential for marketing.

Whether you have already joined or are thinking about joining, make sure you don't make any of these mistakes:

Mistake #1: Not Having a Strategy That is Goal Driven

Instagram offers a way for businesses to use photographs and videos to tell their story. It is the ideal channel for those who want to show off their product or service in real time or show a series of photographs that showcase their manufacturing process. Some even choose to use video as a way of answering frequently asked questions. The possibilities are pretty much endless on Instagram but if you truly want to make the most out of it, you must define your goals right from the start.

An example of who is using Instagram in the right way is a company called Quest Nutrition. They are a popular nutrition company, focused on the low carb and fitness world. Their products are food and drink that are designed to help people reach their goals and their followers grow by approximately 15,000 every month. They do it by using Instagram to engage fully with their audience and make them feel as though they are a part of the company.

Mistake #2: Not Being Focused on Quality

While having a strategy that is goal driven is important, so is the quality of your content. Poor quality videos and photos could mean failure, as people are not interested in looking at what they can't see or hear properly. Think for a minute about how Instagram works. Users looks through columns of photos, quickly reading captions. They only slow and stop when something outstanding catches their eye.

Another time, they may be looking for content through hashtags or scrolling through hundreds of videos or photos until something shouts at them to stop and look. The more you focus your efforts on quality, the more likely users are to want to look at your content and that means they are engaging with you on some level. Compared to the many other social networks posts that go on Instagram tend to stay there for longer. This means that people could be continuing to engage with your content for weeks after you posted it.

Social Media Marketing

Taco Bell is one company that has got this aspect of their marketing campaign down to perfection. On Instagram alone, their followers grow by approximately 6,000 per month and much of this is down to their photography skills. The fast food company does an awesome job of using color and creating an atmosphere that is entertaining and laid back throughout their videos and photos.

They post less than once per day and this approach must be working because they have gained 488,000 followers, 19,000 likes per post and more than 500 comments per post. That is true audience engagement.

Mistake #3: Not Posting Enough

Recent research shows that, on average, brands post an update on Instagram approximately 1 ½ times a day. That same research showed that certain brands posted every hour and saw engagement on their content at above average rates. A big part of your Instagram media campaign that you must pay close attention to is how often you post. Look for a combination of quality and quantity, making sure that you don't sacrifice one for the sake of the other. If your research shows that, you are able to post quality content 10 times a day then you must stick to that posting schedule from then on. Not being consistent in your posting can easily lose you followers and that equates to a potential loss of business.

MAC Cosmetics are a company brand that has it right. Founded in Toronto in 1984, MAC picks up approximately 231,000 new followers on Instagram every month. A single post of theirs garners 34,000 likes and more than 300 comments. Their follower numbers are close to 3 million and that is because they post frequently and consistently. Every day, they post several updates and every update is quality.

Mistake #4: Misusing Hashtags

Yes it is very easy to misuse hashtags on Instagram, whether it be that you are not using enough, using too many or not using the right ones. Hashtags are important in that they help people to discover you on Instagram. Those brands that are not quite so well known or who have low follower counts can make use of popular hashtags that are relevant to their industry to help their content gain exposure. Hashtags can also help you to build up awareness of your brand so consider using them as part of your strategy.

A study has shown that posts that have 11 or more hashtags received around 80% interaction while those using 10 picked up 22% and 41% for 2. Instagram limits you to 30 per post. There is also a direct link between hashtags and comments, likes and followers. However, do not misuse hashtags just to get exposure because it will backfire on you and you will lose credibility. So keep hashtags relevant.

One company that has got hashtag use down to a fine art is GoPro. They make an action camera, the most popular action camera in the world. Their Instagram followers rise by 221,000 every month and they are, quite simply, one of the top brands in the media network. They have more than 4.3 million followers and, if they wanted to, they could probably drop the use of hashtags and not notice any difference. But they choose to leverage this mechanism and it is just one of the reasons why they are so popular on Instagram.

Mistake #5: Buying Followers

This is big business; look anywhere on the net, on freelance sites etc. and you will find people offering to pay for so many Facebook likes, Twitter or Instagram followers. If you can't be bothered to spend the time and effort it takes to build up your following, you probably shouldn't be in business in the first place. Not only that, Instagram is now cracking down hard on fake accounts and they are removing them in unprecedented numbers. On the whole, Instagram engagement rates are on the rise and the best way to tap into this is through quality content and consistent updates.

Nike is a multinational company, one we've all heard of and they are often highlighted for the way they advertise their products. They have almost 13 million followers on Instagram alone; each of their posts picks up around 128,000 likes and more than 900 comments on average. On top of that, their following on the social media channel increases by approximately 1 million every month. They post less than once a day but what they do post is compelling, quality and creative. Their ability to connect with their audience in this way has earned them the right to be one of the most popular brands on Instagram.

Mistake #6: Not Maximizing Your Following

Instagram users like their branded content and they are consuming it at unprecedented rates. However, just because your followers are engaged today, it doesn't mean they will still be there tomorrow. The way to keep them is in how you leverage and interact with them. One of the most effective ways is to promote content that is user generated. Run photo contests, encourage the use of a branded hashtag, however you do it, you are building up real relationships with real people. Give your followers all they need to spread the word about you and share what you post; get your followers working for you.

BarkBox is a company that provides a monthly surprise package for dogs. Their packages include treats, toys and other goodies and 10% of their profits go to different charities. They have already been responsible for the rescue of 800 puppies and can now boast close to 32,000 new followers every single month on Instagram. They are funny and they are entertaining and this is what has helped them to grow their following and promote their cause.

Mistake #7: Being Too Promotional

There is nothing worse than brands posting nothing but posts that are self-promoting. All you see are updates that ask you to buy this, get free shipping, join our sale, etc. This kind of post comes over as being lazy, selfish and, in some cases, distasteful and inappropriate. There is a time and a place to promote your business and it isn't every hour of every day.

Ben and Jerry's are a popular ice cream company and their Instagram following grows by around 14,000 every month. They don't post pictures of ice cream every single day. Instead, they use fan photos on their updates. Getting people to take their own photographs with your product is one very good way of engaging your followers and, for Ben and Jerry's, it works so well, they average 20,000 likes per photo.

Mistake #8: Not being Sold on Instagram

To be fair, there are a lot of social media channels to choose from and you could be forgiven for wondering if you really have the time to manage yet another one or if it is even worth the hassle of joining if your products are not photo-friendly. You are not alone if the real question you are asking is whether Instagram really has a place in your social media marketing strategy.

According to recent research, 38% of marketers do not see Instagram as important and a further 20% said it was only a little important. It is one of the fastest growing social media channels though and, as such, it is very difficult to ignore the value it can have. Within five years, Instagram has grown to more than 300 million users who, each day, share around 70 million photos while liking 2.5 billion more.

General Electric gets the value of Instagram. They are a power, water, gas, oil and energy management company, as well as being involved in aviation, transportation, healthcare and Capital Corporation. Their followers grow by 2,000 per month on Instagram and, while they may not be the first company, you think of, they know how to leverage social media to work to their advantage.

So, over the last four to five years, Instagram has grown from a channel that was used for selfies and pictures of food to one that is being wholly leveraged by brands to deliver a message and engage with real people on real levels. The ones who get the most out of Instagram are those who post content that is of high quality, is engaging, interesting and is posted with a real purpose in mind. That should be you.

Chapter 11
Pinterest

Pinterest is different from Instagram because it started as a picture bookmarking site. Users can pin any picture they come across on the web and all the pictures don't have to be created by them. Users can also create boards for different categories where they can pin the relevant pictures. So someone can have a board for product pictures while another one for cute cat pictures!

Pinterest has over 70 million users but it is much more powerful for marketers than Instagram. A deciding factor whether you should use Pinterest or not can be that over 80% of Pinterest users are female. So if your target audience is primarily female then Pinterest is the perfect match for you.

While the pictures on Instagram tend to be more artistic and creative, the pictures on Pinterest are more glamorous and professional. There is no place for bad or unprofessional pictures on Pinterest. Because users can pin pictures to their boards that they haven't created themselves, Pinterest allows non professional photographers/graphic designers to dress up their boards with high quality pictures.

Pictures of food, art and craft, DIY projects, fitness, fashion, celebrities, cute animals etc. all are present on Pinterest. Users create several boards based on the categories they like and then spend hours pinning pictures from the internet to their boards. Users can also follow other boards. Some boards allow followers to post their own pictures.

Infographics also do well on Pinterest. Because this is such a visual site, visually appealing written content, in the form of well designed infographics, stands out. People share recipes, diet plans, exercise routines, DIY instructions etc. through infographics. Marketers also make good use of infographics.

Another favorite type of content on Pinterest is motivational pictures. These can be pictures with motivational messages or famous quotes. Such posters are also popular on this site.

Success Tips for Pinterest

All the basic rules of social media marketing apply to Pinterest as well. So keep your brand image in mind while creating your page and while posting content. Keep the content valuable to your followers and genuinely interact with them. Follow the 80/20 rule and create 80% content for genuine interaction and entertainment. And offer sales pitches only 20% of the time.

Social Media Marketing

On Pinterest you can create several boards based on different categories. These categories will depend on the kind of business you have. You can have a board for product images, behind the scenes, personal images etc. You can also have fun boards such as cute animals or memes. You don't have to stick to categories that are somehow related to your products. Real people on Pinterest have all sorts of unrelated boards and so should brands and businesses.

The interface of Pinterest suits images in the portrait mode. So make your images vertical rectangles with the width smaller than the length. Ideal size is 730 x 1200 pixels. This is why infographics do well on Pinterest. On other sites where the landscape mode is preferred, infographics are either cropped from top and bottom or are shown with empty strips on the sides.

Use the description portion of the pins wisely. Use keywords specific to your niche and write interesting copy that will attract viewers.

A great thing about Pinterest is that **you don't have to create all original content.** You can repin pictures from other users. Use this great tool to never be short of content. Find and curate interesting pictures that fit your niche or industry. This is why individuals and small businesses, who are starting out in the social media marketing world, can do well to begin with Pinterest. You can find high quality content for your boards without spending too much time or money on it. If you are a big business and can afford it, then do invest in professional photography for your Pinterest account.

You can also repin your old pins. This is great to bring old content back in front of new followers who might never have seen the old pins. All these features make Pinterest the easiest to keep producing high quality content.

Pin consistently and as often as you can. 20 to 25 pins a day is the best number to aim for but if you can't do it consistently over time then stick to 8 to 10 pins a day. The high number of pins shared per day is because of the ease with which you can repin pictures. Make full use of it.

Find a group board in your niche and become a contributor. Group boards are great to establish yourself as a popular account in that niche and grow your audience. Group boards are like guest blogging. Find a place where your prospective customers are and become a contributor. Share your best content there and attract new followers to your own profile.

Verify your Pinterest profile to increase trust, especially if yours is a business account.

Use Rich Pins to create more engaging content. You can create product, recipe, or articles through rich pins. It lets you add extra content to the pin without having to add too much text to your pictures. Product pins will even allow you to add price and link to the store so people can go to the store directly from Pinterest. This shows that Pinterest is focused towards attracting businesses to its site. It's a great place for marketing and it should be a part of any social media marketer's strategy.

If your website has a lot of visual content, **add the Pin It button to your website** so people can share your content on their boards. When someone clicks on that picture they will be taken to your website. A great way to get traffic to your website.

Ask fans to create content for your boards and repin the images they come up with. This is a good way to make sure that you never run out of content to post.

On Google+ and Facebook you can add "pin it for later" links in your long posts. This is a great way to make two social media networks work well together. How this works is that you create a blog post or article on your blog and you also create an interesting image to use on Pinterest. Create a rich article pin using this image or just provide a link in the description. Next create a long post on Facebook or Google+ with the same image as the one used on Pinterest. Don't post the complete article on these sites and just provide a teaser and mention the main points of the article. At the bottom of this teaser provide two links. A "read more" link to your blog page and a "pin it for later" link to your pin on Pinterest. This way you offer a choice to the viewer and increase your followers on Pinterest.

Add a screenshot of your boards or popular pins in your email newsletter. Add a link to this image that will take the email subscribers to your Pinterest profile. This is a good way to turn your email subscribers into Pinterest followers.

If you are active on YouTube or Vimeo, you can also pin your videos on Pinterest and drive extra traffic to your videos.

9 Social Media Mistakes on Pinterest

Pinterest is somewhat similar to a glossy magazine but it is personalized to you and, of course, it is online. It's a fantastic way for people to locate products that they like, organize them how they want them and then share them with other people. As well as that, Pinterest users also buy the products they talk about as well. 69% of people who have visited Pinterest have found something they either want to purchase or already have – compare that to just 40% for Facebook users.

As a person who is marketing their business, Pinterest represents some incredible opportunities. Successful brands use Pinterest to connect with consumers and they create posts that are engaging, liked and repined by their followers. If you get this right, it can supercharge your marketing success across all of your social networks.

Get it wrong and you'll be nothing more than a pin in a very large haystack. No one will know whom you are, where you are, they won't buy from you and they will call you out as a marketer who has no idea what they are doing. Pinterest is the fourth most popular social media channel and if you don't have a clue what you are doing then there is a good chance that you will be making at least one of the following nine common Pinterest mistakes:

Mistake #1: Only Pinning Your Own Products

It's a bit like only talking about yourself or promoting your own products on other social media sites – this is a big no-no. The idea behind marketing on social media sites is that it's meant to be social. You need to interact and engage with your market and relate to your customers and followers in a personable manner. It's all about dialogue, not monologue. Pinning only your own products is liable to see you lose followers and your pins will not be repined.

At the end of the day, consumers are just as busy as business owners are and many use Pinterest as a bit of a distraction when they want a break. Pins that they can identify with, on an emotional level are more likely to get repined. Do not pin loads of images of your own products and certainly don't pin any with wording on like "Buy This!"

Mistake #2: Not Completing your Business Profile Fully

Make sure that your Pinterest account is listed as a business account and make sure that your business profile is fully completed. The same as it is for every other social media site, there is a big difference between a personal Pinterest account and a business one. Having a proper business account will make your company look professional and give it some credibility.

Social Media Marketing

Complete every section in your profile and add a link to your website as well. Use your brand's logo so that people can identify you easily and fill in the "About" section wisely – tell your story, who you are, where you came from and what prompted you to start your business. If you already have a personal account, Pinterest will let you convert it to a business one so you don't have any more excuses.

Mistake #3: Not Including Prices

Including prices on your pins will get you more likes and more followers. 36% more to be precise. It's an easy enough thing to do. Whenever you post a pin, make sure the price is included in the description or, if you want to be really creative, you could include the price on the pinned image.

Mistake #4: Not Making Your Content Engaging Enough

If you really want to post engaging content, go for promotions and contests, and yes, these work just as well on Pinterest as they do on other social media sites. "Pin it to Win it" contests are very popular. And promote it not only to your followers but to their followers as well, and so on.

Mistake #5: Not Linking to Your Product Pages

This is one of the most common mistakes, businesses pinning products without linking back to a product page. It's a complete waste of your time and a golden opportunity missed. The whole point of marketing your business on Pinterest is to get your pins repinned. This means that your pins are being shared and people get to see your products without having to visit your website or your Pinterest home page to see what it's all about. Don't make this simple mistake, always include a link to your product page with every pin.

Mistake #6: Not Describing Your Images

You might think that a picture speaks for itself but when something is taken out of context or you just post random images with no descriptions, people don't know what it is all about. And, if you don't add a description to your pins, they won't be discoverable in a Pinterest search and, if that's the case, why bother being on there in the first place? Make sure you use a good description and include hashtags to make sure your pins are even more discoverable.

Mistake #7: Using Bad Quality Images

Pinterest is all about images and using bad images is a bad move. You are in competition on Pinterest against some of the best images in the world and if yours are not appealing or of really poor quality, don't waste your time in posting them. Your images must not be bland, or uninspiring; they must be motivating and make people want to share them.

You may need to hire a professional photographer or a graphic designer who has a keen eye for marketing, to help you. Or you may have to find the time to develop a new skill of your own. However you do it, if you really want to be effective on Pinterest, you must provide images that conjure up an emotion in your followers, enough to get them to share your pins.

Mistake #8: Not Using Pinterest Analytics

Pinterest provides a set of analytic tools for people to use and a big mistake is in ignoring them. They are free and they are easy to use; so use them. Pinterest Analytics allow you to monitor your boards and test your pins and repins. You can see graphs that break down into specific categories, so you can see what works and what doesn't. You can use them to tweak your strategies to get them right and keep on making improvements until you have a formula that really works.

Mistake #9: Not Keeping Up With Your Pinterest Profile

This should be something that is obvious to everyone but if you do set yourself up with a profile on a social media site, make sure you keep up with it. So many people do this; they get started, they go through all the hoops of setting up their profile carefully and then just forget about it. Many of them don't even deactivate their accounts when they leave and that leaves a bad taste in a lot of mouths, especially if you have a fair number of followers.

Take one huge name – Barnes and Noble. They set up a Pinterest profile, they had six boards and seven pins and they even followed 67 pinners. Now they've stopped pinning and they left 500 followers wondering where they had gone and what happened.

Social media sites are like children or pets; they need constant attention. You can't just abandon them to their own devices; it doesn't work. It will take time to get things going and it may take a few months to gain the traction you want but it is worth all the time and effort. And if things really are not working then sure you can leave the site, but make sure you tell all your followers and deactivate your account as well.

So, now you know how not to use your Pinterest account and how not to get lost among all the pinners out there. Use everything at your disposal to improve your marketing strategies and keep working at it. One day, it will all fall together nicely.

Chapter 12
Other Social Networks

In the last few chapters we've covered the most popular social media networks that you'd want to be on. But these are by no means the be-all-end-all of social media marketing. There are plenty of other networks and social media websites that you can use to market your brand. And new ones come up everyday! In this chapter we'll look at some of these sites that you should consider while building your social media strategy.

Reddit

Reddit is "The front page of the internet." It is basically a link sharing platform where users share links to articles, videos, pictures etc. that they find on the internet. Other users can then upvote or downvote the link based on what they feel about it. If a post gets to the front page of Reddit, it can get a lot of visitors in a short amount of time. Users can also comment on posts and have a discussion on that topic. Comments can also be upvoted and downvoted.

Reddit is not usually considered by marketers and brands because it doesn't take kindly to marketers. The Reddit community despises spammers and marketers and will downvote any post they think is promotional. Brands have in the past faced the wrath of the community. But there are a few savvy marketers who know how to market on Reddit.

In the very beginning of this book I talked about the core principle of social media marketing; always provide value to the followers. A lot of engaging content jabs and very few sales pitch right hooks. This is true most of all for Reddit. If you don't want to spend the time it takes to genuinely participate in the Reddit community, you should avoid it.

How to Market on Reddit?

But if you have the time and willingness to genuinely connect with the community then there are ways to create a presence on the site. Here's how to go about it in a series of steps:

Reddit is divided into subreddits which cater to one particular topic or niche. Find and subscribe to subreddits related to your niche and interests.

Social Media Marketing

Go through these subreddits and find interesting posts.

Read the posts and upvote those you think are worthy of being voted up. Don't downvote just because you don't agree with the author of the post. Downvote if you think the post is irrelevant or simply bad.

Comment on posts, read other's comments, upvote and downvote comments and basically participate in the community.

You must already be reading a lot of articles and watching videos related to your industry or niche. Install the Reddit extension for your browser and share links of these articles in the appropriate subreddits.

Share your own blog posts or articles but don't overdo it. If you share too many links from the same website, you'll be considered a spammer or promoter and your account might even be banned. Share 1 of your own post for at least 9 posts of other websites.

When your links and comments get upvoted you'll earn Karma. It will help you become a leading member of the community. Once you achieve this status in the community your links, whether to your own site or other's site, will be well received.

All this sounds too much work but there is a lot of high quality traffic to be had from Reddit if you genuinely contribute to the community.

If you'd like a simpler plan, you can just buy a sponsored post. It is like buying a banner ad and can lead to an increase in traffic to your website. But if you are willing to do the hard work, you can benefit a lot from genuinely using Reddit.

Clearly, Reddit is not for every marketer. It requires a significant investment of time. You can also try other social discovery networks such as Digg and StumbleUpon to bring your content in front of new viewers. But it is hard to get to the front page of these sites unless you already have a good following on your blog and other social networks.

Scribd

Scribd has over 80 million users worldwide, which makes it a great place for sharing written content. Mostly Scribd is an ebook library of sorts. Users subscribe for a monthly fee and can read as many books as they want. The publishers of the books get royalty based on how much of their book was read by the user. To be a part of this subscription service you need to publish your books with a publisher that is a partner with Scribd. For self-published authors you need to go through Smashwords, Inscribed Digital, BookBaby or Draft2Digital to have your work show up on Scribd.

You can also sell your books on the Scribd store. The users will only be able to view a preview of the book and will have to buy the book in order to read it fully. These two options are for those who have ebooks to sell and want to reach a wide audience.

But there is also a way to market your content for free. You can upload any document and make it available for free to users of Scribd. You won't earn any royalties but you can reach a wide audience. If you have academic papers, white papers, studies, manifestos etc. you can share them on Scribd for free. Add appropriate tags and use your existing social media connections to spread the word.

You can use Scribd to position yourself as an expert in your industry. You can also connect with other industry leaders and build strong relationships.

Slideshare

Slideshare has 60 million users and was acquired by LinkedIn in 2012. It is a site that allows you to share presentation slides. Slides are great for sharing information in an interesting and visually appealing way. A lot of people would rather see a series of visually appealing slides with minimum text than read a lengthy article.

Slideshare is used a lot by professionals researching a topic for work. Other users also come looking for information on a variety of topics. The great thing about Slideshare is that you can have a lead generation form at the end of your slide. So if you are a business and want to pitch your service or product to customers, Slideshare will allow you to do it through a presentation and even let you generate leads directly from the site. This is why there are more businesses and professionals using Slideshare than even Facebook.

It is a great platform for generating leads but it can also come in handy to market your content. You can rehash your written content in the form of a presentation and get more viewers for your content. As always, keep in mind the basic principle of providing value to your audience.

Your slides need to be informative while being entertaining. Don't have too much text on your slides. To make a good presentation you need to tell a story through visuals and as few words as possible. Create a strong headline and an attention grabbing first slide. If you aren't good at design, pay a professional to come with good visuals and typography to create professional slides.

You can embed your presentation directly on your website as well. Share your presentation on other social networks. LinkedIn owns Slideshare and is the best place to share your slides to increase your authority in your niche.

TripAdvisor

TripAdvisor is a travel website that tells users where to stay, where to eat etc. in their favorite destinations. If you have a small restaurant, diner, hotel, homestay etc. you can use TripAdvisor to get significant increase in your business without spending any money. More than 260 million users search for hotels and restaurants on TripAdvisor every month. To get in front of these people you need to list your establishment on TripAdvisor.

People can then find you on TripAdvisor and decide if they want to use your services. If you have a good rating and good reviews, it can bring you a lot of business without spending a dime on any advertising.

To rank high, the most important thing is of course to provide great service. Add lots of pictures of your services. Users are more likely to book rooms in a hotel if they can see the pictures of the rooms in advance. Ask your guests to leave a review on TripAdvisor. More reviews mean one off bad reviews will not dent your reputation too much.

Learn from the reviews. Good reviews tell you what you do well and you need to keep doing that, but bad reviews are more important because they tell you what you are doing wrong. Learn from these reviews and always respond to both good and bad reviews. Thank those who leave a good review and apologize to anyone who leaves a bad review. If you handle a negative review well, it can actually improve your reputation in the eyes of the users.

Commenting on reviews also shows that you actively engage with your guests. You should use TripAdvisor along with other social media networks to provide a comprehensive customer service to your guests.

You can also advertise on TripAdvisor if you want to spend money to get new customers. This is a good option if you are just starting out and don't have much reviews. TripConnect is another service for businesses offered by TripAdvisor. If you choose this service, users can click through to your online booking page directly from TripAdvisor. You have to pay per click and it can be a good strategy to generate business.

Snapchat

Snapchat is an up and coming social network with the differentiating factor that your content is available only for a few seconds after you post it. After that it disappears.

Snapchat has earned a bad reputation as an immature social network because a lot of the content shared on it is, for a lack of better words, immature. With the

Social Media Marketing

promise that the content will disappear in a few seconds, Snapchat encourages people to share content that they won't share on other social networks.

Snapchat has taken the entire philosophy of social networks and turned it on its head. We heard so many news stories where what someone had posted on social media in the past came back to haunt them. It was said that one should always be careful what they post on the internet because it never goes away. But Snapchat has changed that.

Now that the network is growing up, a lot of celebrities have started embracing Snapchat. Their followers eagerly wait for a glimpse from the life of their favorite celebrity in the form of a picture or a video.

The network is so new that there aren't any clear strategies as to how it could be used for marketing. But it does seem to be one of the social networks that is on the verge of breaking into the big leagues. So if you are a social media marketer, you should take a look at it and find out a way to market your product on it. Keep in mind that the demographic on this site skews young. So if your products are for teenagers, you should definitely be on this site, learning how to use it.

In the end, I would like to say that there will always be new social networks coming up. Who knows, maybe one day a new network will even overthrow Facebook as the leader in social media. The world of social networking changes very quickly. As a social media marketer it can seem overwhelming to stay on top of all of this. But you have to remember that as long as you spend some time understanding how a network is used by normal people, and you keep in mind the golden rule to provide value to your followers, then you can never go wrong.

Final Word on Social Media Marketing Mistakes

We now know that social media is one of the most popular forms of online activity and is one of the best tools in your marketing strategy bag. Given that 90% or more of businesses now use social media to market their products or services, you should be in there with them. Anyone who isn't, is missing out on the biggest opportunity they will ever have to make their business a true success.

But, just going through the motions of opening an account or sending out a tweet or two is not enough to guarantee success and if that's all you are going to do, forget about it and don't waste time – yours or other people's. To help you along, the following are 7 social media marketing mistakes that you should avoid making at all costs:

1. Not Building a Marketing Strategy

Believe it or not, fewer than 20% of businesses can say that they have a mature social media strategy. Those that don't have one, can't ever hope to cut through all the information that social media users are faced with every day and they can't ever hope to deliver a message that is effective and engaging.

Creating a social media strategy should be your very first step and must include having goals that are measurable and distinct. You must also have a very clear policy for your social media strategies with clear end goals. Without this, your business can create what is potentially the best content ever but it will make no difference at all.

2. Not Integrating Your Social Media Accounts

Your social media accounts are not little islands. They are not to be left as standalone accounts, as many businesses have found out to their cost. All of your accounts should be integrated together, linked through your profiles and tied in to email addresses, websites and paid search advertising. Not connecting them together reduces the reach that each one has on its own.

3. Twitter – Not Using Pictures

If you use images on your tweets, they take up more space and they help to drive post engagement. Tweets that have an image with them are 200% more likely to be engaged with than a plain old text tweet. You don't need to use an image with every single one but you should use one wherever possible.

4. Twitter - Not Keeping Your voice Consistent

If you have a business account on Twitter, keep it for business use. The same goes with personal accounts, keep them for personal business. While it may seem that using personal anecdotes and chatty messages on your business

Social Media Marketing

account can make you seem a little more real, getting into arguments, using the account to advance activities that are not related to your business or insulting others will do you no good at all. On the other hand, you shouldn't sound as if everything has been produced by a robot, either. Find a happy medium and keep your voice consistent.

5. Facebook – Using the Wrong Sized Image or Not Using One At All

Visual content helps people to engage with content. More than 40% of people say that they respond more positively to images than they do to plain text. Photos get up to 50% more impressions on Facebook than any other type of content and they also get more likes and more comments.

Using an image is one thing; using the right size is another altogether. The image size will vary, depending on where and what it is being used for but, on an average post, the image should be 1200 x 1200 pixels. Ads have different guidelines which you will be notified of when you create an ad.

6. Facebook – Leaving URL's in a Post

If you want to share a link use the link post to do it. Facebook automatically turns that link into an image or video that is clickable. Because of this, you do not need to include any URL's in your posts. While it doesn't do any real harm to have it there, it does give the impression that the business doesn't really understand what Facebook can do. Delete it.

7. Facebook – Not Interacting With Your Followers

This is a common mistake and one that any people make. The idea behind social media is that it is social and interactive. Customers expect you to respond to comments that they make, whether it is to answer a question or just to thank them for commenting. Where complaints are concerned, consumers feel as though they are more connected when their complaints are dealt with efficiently.

Every business that uses Facebook should have a strategy in place for dealing with comments on posts, whether they are negative or positive. Not every comment will need a response so use your own intuition to know.

All brands should be striving to create a voice on social media sites while trying to optimize their efforts by staying away from the mistakes we have talked about in this book.

Part 3

Managing Your Social Media Strategy

Chapter 13
Management

Finally we have begun the last part of our journey. I have talked about 12 social networks and websites and how to get the most out of them. There are several other websites to choose from and new ones are launched every month. The social media world is always changing. Big sites such as MySpace and Orkut have slowly faded away while new ones have taken their place. Other sites like Facebook and Twitter seem to be too big to fail. But you can never be sure what will happen in the future and that's why one key of being a powerful social media marketer is to be adaptable.

To end this exhaustive discussion on social media, I want to talk about how to execute and manage all these various networks without sacrificing all of your time on it.

Evernote

By now you have a strong social media strategy in place. You have a website and a blog. You have chosen the best social networks based on the type of your content and your target audience. You have optimized your profiles according to your brand image and have created valuable content.

But when you start executing your strategy, you'll quickly realize that it can get overwhelming very soon. With so many networks and online presence you need to have a solid management system in place. There are various ways to manage your strategy but I'd like to mention one particular service; **Evernote**.

Evernote is a powerful management tool. The secret to its power is that it doesn't force any management philosophy on you. It is like a blank canvas. You can use your management principles and apply them through Evernote. This allows you to shape it into the perfect tool for your own style of management. It doesn't force you to use it in one particular way and instead allows you full freedom as to how you want to use it.

It is also easy to sync Evernote content between your various devices such as you laptop, phone and/or tablet, which allows you to always stay in touch with your management system no matter where you are.

How to Use Evernote to Manage Your Social Media Strategy

Social Media Marketing

This is an example of a system that you can create to manage your social media strategy. You can adapt it to suit your own needs or create a completely new one of your own.

Start by creating a notebook stack called "Social Media" or something like that. This will contain various notebooks, each one related to one social network that you have chosen to participate in. So it should contain notebooks such as Twitter, Facebook, Slideshare, LinkedIn etc.

Each notebook will contain various notes depending on the social network. One note each notebook should contain is "strategy". This note will outline the strategy for that particular social network. It should contain:

- The name of the social network.

- The name of your brand.

- Your brand image explained in a few words. What kind of tone do you want to use? What kind of cover image and profile image do you need to use? What color palate can you use?

- The goal you want to achieve on that network. Do you want to generate leads for your business or provide customer service? Do you want to generate traffic for your website or sell products? A clear goal will help you create meaningful content for that network.

- Type of primary content you want to share on that network. Talk a bit about your content strategy here.

- What desired action do you want the user to take? Do you want them to click on your links and visit your website? Do you want them to subscribe to your newsletter?

- How is this network linked to your other networks? Do you auto post your tweets to Facebook? Do you share pins on Google+?

- And finally an editorial plan. How often are you going to post content? At what times?

This note will be updated often and you should keep coming back to it in order to make sure that you are sticking with your strategy.

Other notes in each notebook can contain various items. It all depends on the network and how you want to use it. For example, you can have a note in the Twitter notebook where you write down tweets that you want to post throughout the day. At the end of the day you can add all of these tweets to a scheduling app like Buffer. We'll talk about Buffer and other automation tools in the next chapter.

Social Media Marketing

You can create a notebook titled "Resources" and clip articles, pictures etc. that you find interesting or useful that you can refer later. You can also use Evernote to write blog posts and edit pictures using the annotations tool or the Evernote Skitch app. You can share your notes directly on your social networks. You can share notebooks with other people. So if you are working with a team on your company's social media strategy, you can share the notebooks with your team members, and everyone will stay up to date with what is going on.

You can create a checklist for your blog posts. It can be something like this:

- Write first draft

- Edit draft

- Find pictures for post

- Schedule post

- Create preview posts for Google+, Facebook, Pinterest etc.

- Share links to post on social networks

- Schedule future social network posts after a week

Creating such checklists can help you in managing your system.

Then you can also create a notebook for the overall editorial calendar. If your blog is your major source of content then its editorial calendar will be your main calendar. Create a table inside a note that lists the posts that you are going to create in the coming month. Have checkboxes for each social network that you are going to share these posts on. Once you post them on those networks you can check these boxes. This will help you get an overall view of what is going on in your social media marketing strategy. It will let you know what you need to do and when.

Once you start using Evernote you'll find unique ways to use it to make things easier for yourself. There are many other management apps and tools out there. Like Trello and Taasky etc. If you already have a tool, use that to manage your system. If you don't use any tool, start using one because managing a good social media strategy requires the need of such tools that'll help you stay on top of the game. Otherwise things can get overwhelming too soon.

Chapter 14

Automation

The easiest way to manage your system is to automate as much of it as you can. A lot of social networks offer automatic updates to other social networks but this is not always the best strategy to use. If you link all your accounts to every other account, you can create a domino effect where you tweet a link to your blog post and then you tweet a link to the Facebook post that links to the same blog post and then your tweets are posted on Facebook and Facebook posts are posted on G+ and so on and so forth. All this happens instantly as soon as you publish your post and this shows carelessness as you are filling up your viewers' timelines with the same content over and over again.

Instead you need social media management apps. Through these apps you can schedule posts on almost all of your social networks. You can create several posts that are tailored for that particular network. The post that works on Twitter will be completely different from what you should post on Facebook or Google+. Let's talk about some of these apps now.

HootSuite

Hootsuite is an app that lets you control several different social media platforms from one page. You can add sites like Twitter, Facebook, G+ (but only business pages), LinkedIn and even wordpress. The ability to control wordpress means that if your blog is on wordpress, you can post content directly from your HootSuite dashboard. This makes managing all of your social networks an easy job. You can use it on your laptop and your phone both. Which means that you always stay on top of your social media.

You can organize all the different social networks in tabs and even add separate streams for separate content. For example, you can have one stream for Twitter mentions, one stream for Twitter retweets, and one stream for the main Twitter timeline. All this on the Twitter tab. Then you can add a Facebook tab and have different streams within it. For free accounts there is a limit that only three streams can be opened on one tab. But you can get over this limitation simply by opening several tabs for the same social network.

If you are a serious marketer and have a lot of social networks, consider getting the paid version of HootSuite for the extra functionality. But even in the free version you can create a message in one place and post it in different social networks. You can schedule posts on different networks. You can also shorten links at a click which comes in handy while tweeting. Paid accounts can create customized shortened links. So instead of a generic "Ow.ly" link you can create a link like "Buy.Now" link.

You can create reports based on the analytics that are provided by HootSuite. It will automatically track data on shortened links. Free accounts have a limit to how many reports they can create. You can even have these reports emailed to you everyday or every week. You can also buy apps for HootSuite that let you connect more social networks including Gmail, YouTube, Instagram etc.

HootSuite is powerful and has a minimalist design which makes it easy to stay organized. It takes some time to learn all that you can do on this app but once you learn it, it can become your best friend as a social media marketer. If you have a social media team that works together, HootSuite can allow several profiles to use the same dashboard. It is a great way for teams to work together on social media.

Buffer

Buffer started out as an app specifically for scheduling tweets but has now grown to cover other social networks such as Facebook profile, Facebook page, G+ page, LinkedIn Profile, LinkedIn Page etc.

It works similar to HootSuite but has a much different layout. Some will prefer HootSuite's layout while others might prefer Buffer. But the key features that separate Buffer from HootSuite is the browser extension and how well it works with other apps.

You can use Buffer with reading apps such as Feedly and Pockets and share content you find interesting right from your reading app. You can schedule it to be shared on various networks. You can connect Buffer to Followerwonk and use it to automatically schedule posts while most of your followers are online. You can connect URL shortening apps and also get analytics on how many people click on your link.

By purchasing a web browser extension you can share content directly from the web browser. You can even highlight a piece of text that you want to quote and click on the browser extension and it will automatically create a post for you.

Buffer too comes in a free version and a paid version. The free version has limits on how many tweets you can schedule. So if you are serious about your marketing, invest in a paid version of this wonderful app.

SumAll

All social networks now provide detailed analytics for you to improve your content and your posting and marketing strategy. But if you are using an app like HootSuite to post content on all networks from one place, then you don't want to have to go on each individual site to search for analytics. That's where SumAll comes in.

It's an app that lets you view analytics from over 40 social networks in one place. SumAll has also introduced a paid feature called SumAll Insights. These are detailed reports based on your analytics. You can get these PDFs which convert the raw data into meaningful reports for you. They'll tell you how you are performing and also suggest tips to improve your marketing strategy. If you are an individual or a small business that can't afford a team of marketers analyzing data and creating such reports for you, this is certainly something worth investing in. It's ROI will be huge based on how much you can improve your social media marketing strategy.

IFTTT

One of the best ways to automate things on the internet is to use IFTTT.com. This is a wonderful service that stands for **IF This Then That**. You can create your own "recipes" to automate almost anything. You need to define the terms 'This' and 'That'.

So you can say that IF "I post a picture on Instagram" Then "tweet it as a native picture on Twitter." This recipe will post your Instagram pictures on Twitter. If you use the auto sharing service of Instagram the tweet will only contain a link to your Instagram but not the picture. This IFTTT recipe lets you bypass that problem.

There are literally thousands of recipes to choose from or you can create your own recipe that suits your particular need. IFTTT is considered to be the most powerful tool on the internet. The potential is limitless with this tool. It is the best tool for anyone looking to automate their online life. As a social media marketer you should learn to use it. You'll find that a recipe exists already for most things you want to do. And you can borrow them. But to get something specific done, just create a recipe for it.

Here are some inspiring recipes that already exist on IFTTT:

- Daily SMS weather forecast. Get an SMS every morning for the day's weather forcast.

- Wake up call. Get an automated call on your phone as a backup alarm.

Social Media Marketing

- Starred emails in Gmail to Evernote. To send an important email to Evernote so you can read it later, just star it on Gmail and IFTTT will do the rest.

- Reminder SMS for events on Google Calendar. Never forget birthdays, anniversaries, meetings, appointments etc.

- Once a day tweet. Like to say good morning to people everyday on Twitter? Why not automate it?

- Connect any social network with another one.

You get the idea. IFTTT is really the height of automation. It is limited only by your creativity.

Dlvr.it

Dlvr.it is an app that lets you automatically share your blog posts on all of your social networks. We've mentioned earlier that if automatic posting of blog posts is done unwisely, it can do you harm in the long run. But Dlvr.it gives you a lot of options to customize how the posts are shared.

To share posts you need to create 'routes'. Each route contains a source and the destinations where the post will be shared. You can set different routes for different post types, categories etc. on your blog. You can even set routes for RSS feeds of blogs that you like. So when someone shares an article on a blog that you like, it gets shared automatically with your followers.

In the destinations section you can add several social networks like Twitter, Facebook, G+, LinkedIn, Tumblr etc. You can also add separate accounts on one social network. For example if your business has a Twitter account and you also want to share articles on your personal Twitter account then you can add both in the destinations.

Dlvr.it lets you customize how the posts are shared and also let you get analytic data on how each post does. When used wisely, this app can ease the management of your social media strategy.

There are hundreds of apps out there that will give you an advantage in some way while working on social media. You should read blogs that talk about such apps and what's new in the social media world so you are always up to date about what's going on. To stay ahead of the curve you have be even more proactive and look out for new apps, social networks and strategies and be among the first ones to try them. Find the best strategy that works for you and the best apps to help you manage that strategy.

Chapter 15
Outsourcing

The last piece of the puzzle is outsourcing. If you are an individual offering a service or product and after reading this entire book you feel overwhelmed and wonder how you can do all this singlehandedly, then you don't need to get too worried. The best solution is to outsource as much as you can to freelancers.

Freelance Marketplaces

There are some great sites for finding freelancers who can do everything from designing your website, developing an app for your website, writing great copy, writing blog posts, creating stunning visuals, designing your brand, writing ebooks and even managing your social media networks. Hiring freelancers is simply about finding the right candidate for your project and budget. Upwork (formerly oDesk) is one of the biggest and most successful freelance marketplaces. It took over Elance and the two sites have now merged, making Upwork the best place to find good freelancers. Behance, Fiverr etc. are also good sites to find talented freelancers. You can even try looking for freelancers on LinkedIn.

Outsourcing can help you create a social marketing team at a fraction of the cost of hiring locals to work full time for you. Small businesses and individuals have no other option but to go for outsourcing if they want to seriously improve their social media marketing.

Finding Good Freelancers

It takes some time to find good freelancers. You need to put your job ad and then sort through a lot of bids. A good way to sort through them is to look at the ones who have taken time to write a good cover letter for you. Most freelancers will send generic letters and bids. Avoid these and find those who've actually spent some time thinking about your job.

The only way to know for sure if a freelancer is a good fit for you is to work with them. The good thing is that you don't have to hire someone for a lifetime. Just hire for one sample project that doesn't cost much and see how the freelancer performs. Once you find a few freelancers you like you can work with them and see which ones are best for you. Build a long term relationship with a good freelancer. Look for those who can communicate properly because more than technical skills, communication skills decide how the project goes. If the freelancer is proactive in communication, readily available and 'gets' you, then stick with them.

Don't think that all freelancers are part-time workers looking to make a few extra bucks, who possibly can't work seriously on your projects in the long term. There are a lot of professionals who are choosing to work full-time as freelancers. It gives them the freedom to work from anywhere they want and to choose who they work with. So don't be afraid and embrace the freelancing revolution.

The best way to outsource is to hire a Virtual Assistant (VA) to handle your entire social media management. VAs can do almost anything you want them to do. They can organize your content and schedule posts. You can allow them to control your social media networks through an app like HootSuite, where you too can keep an eye on things from your own account. They can even interact with your followers on your behalf, if you want them to.

How to Hire and Train a Good VA

Look in the right places. You can find VAs on most freelancing websites but there are certain websites specifically for VAs like www.assistu.com www.virtualassistantnetworking.com etc.

The profile should be professional and without grammatical and spelling mistakes. Professional VAs will also have a professional website that lists their skills and experience.

Look for the VA with the right skills. If you need someone for social media management, then that person should be experienced with the sites you are active on. They should also be experienced the tools and apps that you use.

Look for VAs with the right amount of experience. More experienced VAs will charge higher so the decision has to be based on your budget. But do not be too miserly and hire the cheapest VA.

A VA offering their service at a very low rate means that they are inexperienced and don't value their own time. Inexperienced VAs will use your time to learn on the job. Although a little bit of time should be allowed for the VA to learn how you work, you don't have to pay while they learn the ropes of the entire business.

Conduct an interview over Skype. Make sure the VA can communicate effectively and has the right mental attitude. More than anything else, you should be able to get along well with each other and also understand each other easily.

In the first few interactions with a VA you can judge how professional they are in terms of replying timely to emails etc.

Social Media Marketing

Set the right expectations from the start. If someone is inexperienced, start them off with a smaller work load. The usual payment method is based on per hour so you only pay for the hours of work put in by the VA.

Train your VA in your system of working. If you are a business, make sure they understand the policies you follow. Set clear boundaries of what the VA can and can't do. Let them have enough independence to take small decisions without bothering you for everything but don't give them so much responsibility that they can't handle it.

When using a VA to handle your social media accounts you have to be extra careful that the VA understands how you want them to interact with your customers. A rude comment by an irritated VA can cost your business dearly. Make sure they know your brand's voice and can use it well.

Finally, **don't hire a VA right in the beginning of your social media marketing campaign**. Wait till you yourself have built a set of processes to streamline your marketing strategy. Only when you understand your processes and have found a way that works for you, can you teach it to your VA.

By automating and outsourcing you can manage a lot of social networks with ease. It's all about the ROI. The more you invest in social media marketing, the more returns you'll see. These tips will help you manage the entire social media system that you have created, with ease. You can focus on your business and let your social media run smoothly on the side without wasting too much time on it.

Conclusion

Thank you again for purchasing this book!

I hope this book was able to help you to understand what social media marketing is all about. I hope you can see that it is not as hard as it can sometimes seem. You just need to follow some general rules of etiquette and you'll be fine. Be honest and be human. Spend time in the social media world and stay abreast with the latest trends. Interact with people and build strong communities. Provide real value to your followers and you can never go wrong in social media.

The next step is to create your own social media strategy by using the right networks for your business. In the beginning start with a handful of sites and as you get good at managing those, add new sites to your network.

Finally, if you enjoyed this book, then I'd like to ask you for a favor, would you be kind enough to leave a review for this book on Amazon? It'd be greatly appreciated!

Click here to leave a review for this book on Amazon!

Thank you and good luck!

M.J. Brown

Made in the USA
Middletown, DE
03 February 2016